Silent Corner

Prof. Keisha R. Miles

10/26/20

Dear Nesha,

Allow the stories, prose, vignettes, poetry, and narratives to be inspired to tap into your own journey of phenomenal strength. In your own young battle scars allow your to become your Super Stars with Self Care. Always on the forefront.

Love you,
Auntie

FOREWARD

By Lupita Samuels

SILENT CORNER, is a mixture of provocative prose and profound poetry, exciting the mind, stimulating the heart, leaving one wanting for more like in a mystery movie. Indeed, it is a mystery and a miracle that Keisha Miles is alive, so she cannot be *silent*.

Professor Keisha Miles exemplifies the meaning of perseverance in the face of adversity. Throughout her late 20's and 30's, the author experienced life-threatening assaults on her health along with extreme hardships in her personal life. Divorce, an ugly custody battle for her beloved children, the loss of her devoted father during the same season, compounded by her health challenges, might have really kept her **"*silent*"** forever, but for Keisha Miles' profound faith coupled with the loving support of family and friends.

Professor Miles' passion for the arts (dancing, acting, directing, choreographing, writing), along with her concern for the total wellbeing of others led to her unique style of teaching. She deftly blends performance and academics in her devotion to helping others as a teacher and Educational Coach, and this is quite evident in her writings.

The author embodies the warrior ethos. Just as she fought for her very survival, repeatedly triumphing over adversity, she fights for the minds and bodies of her young charges, taking the disempowered, the oppressed, the ones least likely to succeed and turning theirs into success stories that mirror her own. Hers is clearly a story to tell. The deep feelings and emotions evoked and expressed in this book will certainly resonate with the sensitive reader who might need a moment of 'silence' to ponder the significance of life in its myriad manifestations.

It is no surprise that Professor Miles is greatly loved and admired by all of us who are privileged to know her.

INTRODUCTION

Let no one tell your story.

There will always be those who will create a platform for their own agenda. I have decided to be the storyteller of my own soul. It has a historical narrative of African Ancestry Southern Roots, Urban Blues, and Hip-Hop news. It has been shaped by some mental challenges triggered by others that I allowed to violate my space without knowing how to control my reaction.

I proudly unveil the three deadly D's that almost killed me. At least I thought so for a second and reality came back for me. His name was my saving grace JC (Jesus Christ). Divorce, Disease, and Depression all attacking my body simultaneously. Triggering factors have a way of hijacking your internal organs, when you're young, talented, black, woman, beautiful, driven, and wounded. I hold no apologies, nor do I make excuses for my existence. It is strong. It is Harriet Tubman Strong. Remember when she got hit in the head by a man, who happened to be a white man, who also happened to be an Overseer of our African American enslaved people. She found something deep in her heart like an unsettling gut feeling after escaping free that she still was not free; until she led and went back to get hundreds of slaves.

In the moment of her decision she realized her husband agenda would not allow that. She had to let him go! Well I was that Harriet with heart injury called broken after my divorce while breast cancer visited me during my custody battle of my children, then followed by a bullet of Breast Cancer three times. Like Harriet I had a bigger mission, because those pretty babies of mind were my freedom. I had to create an underground railroad for them to have a blueprint to escape the scars of abandonment or insaneness. When BC visited me my JC Jesus Christ anointed my steps to rise to dance, to pray, to lead, to teach, to advocate, to coach and to push forth giving birth through the darkness. Not even a man could stop me from being a Freedom Fighter to give my babies life opportunities even when his agenda was MIA, like Harriet Tubman's husband.

This is not about a divorced single black mother abused by her husband who abandoned his children story. Wrong book. However, it is about celebrating a journey of vignettes, corners of life situations, birth, loss, rebirth, and a resurrected death. It will make you cry, laugh, and reflect on the mirror looking back at you called life.

It is a journey. A #KMILESJOURNEY of kilometers steps circumstances fantasy love laughter love making and making love endured especially when held up by strong roots called family. It is like a choreographed dance production infused with politics, love, heartache, history, the historical strength of a black women and men endured, but all coming from black girl of Harlem origin, southern roots, and African Ancestry now all Grown unveiling the *Silent Corner that* needs to be open for healthy dialogue, in order to heal.

A Letter to My Then 17 Year Old Self (1987)

(Picture from Seventeen Magazine)

I am comforted to know that although I walk through the dark, I walk with hope in my heart, knowing that I do not walk alone. Life has a final meaning which resides outside of me. That is in God and my God-given talents. I will not give up. I shall continue to press on through the wind and the storm until that golden star appears at the end of the road.

I know that one day the sun will burst right through the clouds of rejection and cast her golden rays upon me as a spotlight on the stage. Then someone will say, "You are exactly what we've been looking for. Girl — you're right on time!"

Keisha Miles

CONTENTS

Relationships

Black Breast

Revolution Evolution

Streets

#Confirmations

#BlackToo

Dedicated to my loving Parents Catherine and late Rufus Miles Jr.; My late grandparents Caroline Lowe and Elijah Lowe; Addie Miles and Rufus Miles Sr.; my nieces Donashia and Shadonia Dewar and my loving children Imani Bruno Isis R. Bruno.

Prof. Keisha R. Miles

ACKNOWLEDGMENTS

I would like to thank my parents Catherine and Rufus Miles Jr. They provided me with a solid foundation of black self-pride and community activism. Through their support, I was always encouraged as a little girl to tap into my creativity through Education, Writing, Dance, Music, Acting, Modeling, and community service. Whatever gave me a voice and expression of empowerment, I owe it to my family.

A special shout out in heaven to my Aunt Laverne Baker the first African American female accepted into the Boston Conservatory of Dance who was influential in recognizing my dance skills in the crib to make sure I trained professionally at the age of 4.

I am also thankful for the journey of surviving Breast Cancer three times, while raising amazing children who received full academic scholarships to college; my son Imani R. Bruno a recent graduate from University of Virginia with a Mechanical Engineering Degree and my daughter Isis R. Bruno a NYU Dean Scholar and Tisch recipient who attends New York University Tisch School of The Arts majoring in Musical Theatre helped me to inspire to do more. I am blessed to have been given the anointed task to raise my nieces Donashia and Shadonia Dewar who taught me that all things are possible through faith, works, and pushing through.

Thankful for my praying sister Ordained Minister Marcella Miles who has spoiled and loved me from a baby to an adult; thank my loving sisters Brenda Miles, Fay Miles and Jackie Flowers for being part of the journey.

I thank my brother Carl Keith Miles who has always been my soldier, warrior, mentor, stellar math tutor for my children while they were growing up, an amazing Uncle who stepped in financially emotionally as a surrogate dad always for my babies. He has been my bullet proof shield.

I would like to thank my cousin Chevon Miles the artist of my book cover. I sent her my photo and she brought it to life; Justin Hodges and all of his work on my audio book; as well as, the renowned Fashion Designer Ms. Hope Wade Of WWW.HOPEWADEDESIGNS.COM for her regal royal cape of **Black Lives Matter** that I modeled on the back of the book cover.

I would be remiss in my duties if I did not thank Regina Abraham who became my personal coach in saying for years, "It is your time Keisha. You have to sit down and publish your works. You have helped everyone else and encouraged, personally Educational Life Coach them in their careers and educational dreams. Now you must coach and do you." My Aunt Gina was another person who year after year has sat me down and said it is time for you to publish your books. Thankful to my Aunt Gloria, Aunt Janice, and Aunt Lily for your love, support and special experiences that help shape my life.

Lupita Samuels, Professor Pamela D'ambrisia, and Dr. Maria Smith for editing my works. Personal thanks to my Poetry Table Meetup group in the village for allowing me a creative space to share and perform my original works.

Special thanks to my circle of sisters who kept pushing me to publish my works for over the past 20 plus years. There are too many to mention, but some I must. Iris Randelman, and Saffiyah Sharif, with your endless telephone calls of encouragement over the years cheering me on to be fearless to tell my stories because of my God-given gift. I thank my college sister friend Attorney Veronique Pluviose in which we met over 30 plus years in a Black Literature Summer Class course and fell in love with The Song of Solomon by Toni Morrison and with each other. Thank you for creating a sacred creative space for me to always retreat to at your home and for showing me every day through your actions that you love me unconditionally. Always sponsoring me to come to DC to participate in the literary world. Thank you and Charmyn Henderson for being my following as I performed at the DC Poets and Busboys in D.C. and in Maryland, During a very difficult time in my life. Thank you Darlene Brooks-Thomas for sharing your daughter Treasure Brooks with me who gave me more life and our special sisterhood relationship as mothers with similar struggles, accomplishments and common thread success of raising our exceptional children through major sacrifices of mountain and valley top experiences circumstances called life.

Thank you Natasha Lovell-Walker for always being there as my childhood friend and ride or die. Thankful for my Cathedral High School sisters especially Principal Venessa Singleton and Frankie O'Brien for their love and support throughout the journey. Tasha Wray thank you for the many years of keeping me physically fit with Bikram Yoga, ballet bar, pole dance classes and so many fun adventures that restored my sexy and sanity. Kelly Simmons you are one of my oldest friends since nursery school. I thank you for your extended artistic ear listening to my works in the car on a CD as we drove through Manhattan last year on our way to see my daughter Isis perform at NYU, you said, "Girl you have to perform this. This is some good stuff!"

I like to thank my family therapist Ruth Warwick who said, "The little girl in you is silently crying and why does she need to fix everyone problems? Everything in your life right now must be re-channeled energy as an Educational Life Coach to make your dreams a reality like you have been doing for so long for others." I like to thank Dr. Haynes my divorce therapist who said to me when I was 28 years old, "Sometimes you must put your dirty clothes out to air for everyone to see, in order to become cleansed and healed." Shout out to my savvy Family and Divorce Lawyer Joey Jackson for his support and mentorship during a very challenging time in my life.
Special thanks to my Cancer Breast Surgeon Dr. Nella Shapiro, my Cancer Social Worker Gloria Nelson, and Oncologist Dr. Joseph Sporano. They have been my miracle dream team in keeping me healed.

Thankful to my mentor and breast cancer survivor sister Principal Cheryl Lugo for allowing me to be free to create choreograph direct teach through an interdisciplinary approach using Humanities to inspire our children through the performing arts at MS. 113 Richard R. Green. Thank you for help saving my life the day you let me leave early to get my breast checked out. Principal Edith Bly Jenkins you have been cheering me on since I was young to publish and even help tell your story. Thank you for the love and guidance.

Special thanks to my Trinity Baptist Church Extended Family and late Pastor Nathaniel Tyler Lloyd who supported me through my divorce, custody battle, and battles with Breast Cancer three times. They helped with my children and my nieces' spiritual journey.

Thankful for my male cousins Antoine Lowe, Danny Gates, Shawn Miles, Keith Miles, Bertram Barnes, and Timothy Finn who have been part of my wings. Special thanks to my childhood best friend Jesus Rodriguez who has never stop praying and calling me for over 30 plus years. I am thankful for my Godmothers Eurethea Carter and the late Idamae Barnes for extended roots.

I am most thankful for listening to my Creator who constantly spoke to my spirit by repeating to my rhythms, "Believe Keisha Rosina Miles your trials of battle scars and valley moments will be transformed into mountaintop stars to encourage and inspire others to cross over into their purpose, in spite of the journey."

A Black Woman

NANNA GRANDMA

As I look into her secret place
Nana, her deep dark brown eyes gaze into my bosom
I lay into her hands
Weeping into her rag
tied so tight around her head,
so many stories
in that head rag.

DARK,   DUSTY,   CLEANSING

The old stories they tell
When Grandma and Great Grandma
Nana used that rag for blood
Blood that flows through the black girls body in preparation
For childbirth

Blood that kept her color alive
Her soul turn inside out
Contracting outward over
The Rag was
Is the rapture of
The Black Girl

Black Woman Link
To Her Reproduction
Giving
Continuing
To Replenish
New Seeds
Nana Grandma
"TANKS" for the Rag
It could wrap around our bodies at times
Hold our babies on Our Backs
Cover Our Heads like Crowns
          Looking like queens,
Like our Mamas getting ready for the Harvest
                              Wrapping that Rag to Protect
The Over flow the
Birth Canal
                    The bringing forth
Of New Life
Nana Grandmas

Black Girl can now
Survive off the Rag
           The Shero stories
The tears laughter
The Love Endurance
Sometimes covering Our Feet
Wrapped Around Our Ankles
   The Rag Saved Our Generations to Come
Nana Grandma
   Embellished by the Rupture of the Middle Passage
Soul Rhythms of the Earth
The Dirt
The Plantation that Smothered Surrounded and Drowned Us
Could not Execute Our Spirit
Yes Nana Grandma

Of BLACK WOMANHOOD

So Don't You RUN Now Little Black Girl
Cause You Must
Stroke
Contract
Bend
Leap
Walk
Erect through the hell, the darkness
So when Light hits you
You can Embrace Nanas
Grandmas
Rag
And Wrap it Around!!!

MOTHERLESS

Girl Meet It With Force
    Defeat it with Stare
Shake it with Rhythms
    Deflate It With Nakedness

Cause you brown girl
   Ain't got to look in no Freudian
Book
   Just take one look at Your Mama
Her Mama
    And Great-grandmama
If that ain't
Enuff Force
                    Stare
          Rhythms
And Naked Sheer Beauty

I'se just don't Know what is!
Cause Mama could force that lying man
Up a Yonder to Come Falling On His Knees revealing
His wrong doins
    How Grandma could stare you into
Believing
      When you had lost Self

 Great Grand mamma would bring it all home
with her Secret remedies of Ancestral Times
   And Spiritual Rhythms of Praise Dance

 Healing You Back to Breathing Again
    "So don't you Fret no More Child.. Ya Hear Now?"
CAUSE
   All you Gotta do is   Stare
                   Strut
           Shake
     And Wrap the Rhythms tightly to
That Deep Brown
   NAKED SKIN

COMING INTO SEASON

Leaves shedding off
Colors forming
Into
Moods
Arms
Reaching out
Baring All nakedness in Winter,
Showing All Her Deep Shades
Colors of Beauty Illuminating
From the Sun
How the Complexions
The pigmentations of her skin change

From season
Like October Leaves
And Libra Sun

Strong like Woman giving birth
No Matter
What Season
She Stands Erect
Even on her back
Beautifully Erect

Naked
Like the Winter
Clinging to her Roots
Blossoming
During her Transitional Phase
Still Blossoming
Dancing a shallow Dance
When need be
However the Wind Goes

ERECTED

The tree is She.
                It Stands Erected
Strong, singing swaying
Dancing and talking
                Through the Storm
Of   Shallow hurricane
Sharpened sun,
 Fall of colors,
It Stands Erect and Strong.

 It is spiritually
Flowing through you
 Its roots are strong
And its Gravity has
A Devouring Pulling
 Force
It is so gentle, yet Persistent
A branch can fall off and hurt someone
If it has been tampered with
Molested, Abused By Human Nature
Mother Nature will Dismantle
Man's Disregard of this tree Spatial Environment
Just like the music she plays

The tree through its Geometric/Circular/Pelvic
RHYTHMS
Penetrate the SOUL of MAN
  It nurtures, tame,
Heals the body
  The soul of her story
Through the music, multi rhythms it creates
YES The tree is me.
 Strong. Gentle. Erect. Powerful. Spiritual.
     And full of rhythmic tunes Eating at my Spiritual
ROOTS.
      WITHSTANDING IT ALL IN SPITE Of……

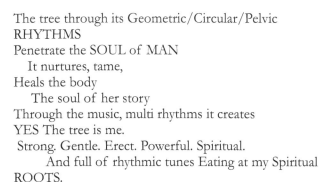

6

SHAKE IT UP

I STRUT
I SHAKE
DANCE
CRY
LOVE

I'SE MAKE LOVE
STRUT
DANCE
CRY
AND LOVE AGAIN

PRAYING ON MY KNEES

EYES TIGHTLY SHUT
BLACK HANDS OPEN
HEART ACHING
TEARS FALLING
SOUL YIELDING
COMPELLING

MIND TOSSING
COMPLAINING SADNESS
EXPLODING
EGO STROKING

SEARCHING
WAILING SCREAMING!
ILLUSION
DELUSION

CONFUSION

HARLEM SUNSHINE

Dancing in her skin
    Hollering through the rhythms
Black Ballerina
    Bare it all

Shake, Leap, Sway
    Weep through your Contractions
Penetrate the Percussions
    Of those curved hips

Look into his eyes as he picks
    Throws, lower you down into
 His arms
    Gracefully wrapping your thighs around his
Essence
    Dancing on your toes
Allowing him to bend you in all
    Positions
Baring Your Beauty
    Black Beauty
        Sparkling through the dim red light

That Pink Ballerina illuminating her
    Blackness on the bare stage
Of Harlem Sunshine
    They look in Awe
How Can that Black Ballerina have Harlem Sunshine on Her Ballet Shoes?
    How can
                That
                   Black Ballerina
                        have
Harlem Sunshine on her Ballet Shoes?
    How can her feet hit the floor sounding
Like drums from Mother Africa?
How can her Arms look like the Circle of Life?
    Only Harlem Sunshine knows

As it is imprinted on her feet!

MODERN WOMAN OF DANCE

Modern woman dancing
To Modern Dance
Ancient rhythms
From motherland
Percussion and Base
Trumpet and Sax
Playing Melodies
Creating Authentic Moves
Storytelling her modern Blues
Southern Roots
Tantalizing feet
Harlem Jazz emphasizing
Movement of hips
Swaying of head
Sharpness of tongue
Chanting Response and Call
Of Ancient African Contractions
Through bosom and back
Classical arms -   in whirlwind
Extend   Bend
Define
Leaping into Place
Rolling up
Releasing out
Modern Woman
Create Modern Dance
Using Ancient Rhythms
Of Motherland
Southern Blues
Of Harlem Jazz
Retrieving Her Story
Through pelvic
Circular
Triangular
Movements in space
RE-DEFINED
MODERN WOMAN
Creates Modern Dance

PROUD BLACK WOMAN

Telling our stories
        Like
Only We can tell
Looking at the images of Oprah
        Viola from southern roots
So
Deeply black
        Rooted in a South just shy of slavery
Tears fill me up
Cause the blood that
Runs through my veins
 I too sing of my pain
 Inspired by
 "America the beautiful
 Beautiful America??"

NOT A SLAVE?

But a beautiful Princess
Who happens to be black?
On the South Carolinian plantation of
Gullah Creole of African Griots
       With shores of
                    Blue
      And clay dirt
Mixed Skin tones of sand
             Pricked by white cotton!

CROWN

Wrap it
Blow it
Knot it up
Straighten it out
Twist it up
Skin it Bald
Fabric wrap
Crochet it
Extend it
Let it be
Roll it up
Bleach it out
Fry it up
Chop it off
Black Hair
Crown Magical
Attitude
Mask unmarked

Entitled to Express
Sassiness confidence her story
instead of their image of beautification smothered by Gentrification

Don't let this straight hair fool you or these braids extended with Afro puffs or locks
Wrap it around as it is worn as your crown

You can't touch it curious by the versatility the diversity the regal ness the culture the pop that hip hops the Urban Southern Caribbean African Roots Gentrification you can neither hold nor wear this crown nor steal it

I know what you're thinking how brainwashed that crown was trying to emulate colonization but the revolution wouldn't allow it the wrap bares her story on her crown

It is mystical it can only be authentically sparked by the essence of
Her   She   Ebony

Sometimes we are taught to hide our curls our thick naps our coarseness cause mirror on the wall said to be the fairest of the ball hot comb it flat iron it perm it fry it pull it out of its natural ecosystem be aware of fire forces on the crown to be buried so deep from its natural habitat but the crown wins

It eventually overpowers the mirror and rebuilds her own reflection of fabulous defining expression of Stunning and just dead fucking Gorgeous

You set the bar the song of lyrical heighten jazz blues all with your crown unbeatable beats genres storytelling it all !!!!

WHITE HAIR

As soon as she comes into their space with her natural hair they start
flipping their hair She notices though at the school in the limited Suburban
urban area with limited thinking
that the black girls' students begin to mirror her as they wear their hair
natural

One colleague audaciously said to her

"You know you can perm your hair" She was biracially mixed or mixed up

Another white woman colleague said you know "men like hair lots of it"
 But her man is the husband who put her in debt with his gambling ways"
was she supposed take advice from her

Her students of color and layers of textures would come to her in pursuit
what to do with my hair?

How to handle it?

You don't handle it you seek knowledge to deal with your natural
textures....
She recalls as it was pouring rain the same mixed up colleague said
"If I go into this rain my hair will turn Chaka Kahn." Throwing shade as
Ms. Brown walked through the doorway

Not knowing Chaka Kahn was Every Woman like she.

Childhood Memories

BLACK BROTHER SOLDIER

I felt so much pride when my big brother surprised me in 7th grade at Our Lady of Grace my parochial elementary school in the North Bronx. He showed up for graduation dressed in his Marine suit over 6 feet tall holding my hands down the street from school. All eyes were on us. He held my hand right as we strolled with a swag, stature, posture three blocks to my house. It was the long walk home with my chest out shoulders pushed back with my face fully smiling teeth showing. This was my brother the Marine. The uniform set the tone. I was 12 years old and you could not tell me I was not a star walking with my soldier.

Then the same feeling I felt in my junior year of high school when my brother took me to his College John Jay to a basketball game. He introduced me as his baby sister and his friend Michael gazed at me. He said "I don't see anything baby about her." I knew then I could not wait to go to College! I ran to a pay phone and called our mom excited about being with my brother at his college and how I anticipated my turn to attend College. Holding on to those two feelings with my brother innocent and happy was simply phenomenal. Like a time you can never get back but never forget. A little sister 6 years younger than her brother looking up to her marine and college student.

I remember at my terror stricken 6 year old face when the gang from 147th street between 7th and 8th avenue tried to jump my brother again. They always thought the kids who lived in Esplanade Garden Co-ops were the haves and they the have nots. I stood in the circle cussing, "Leave my brother alone assholes," with my hands on my hips and rolling my eyes. He came out with his nunchucks like Bruce Lee. Sometimes it was like everyone hates Chris and we would have to marathon Home!

Our journey continues one Saturday when my brother had to pick me up from dance class at Harlem School of the Arts. That particular day he bet to race me home with him on the skateboard and me on foot. He gave me a head start. As I was running across 145th Street and Bradhurst Avenue I was hit by a car went up in the air under the New York City Sanitation garbage truck. As I woke up in Harlem Hospital I could hear the echoing of my Aunt Gloria cussing the staff out about the length of time we were in the ER. I was in first grade that year it was 1976 and remember Sister Vincent coming to my house to homeschool me for a couple of months. All I could think of, that must have been the hardest phone call for my brother to make home.

16

DADDY TEA

Daddy thank you for the tea
Oh how I savor the root from the tree
Daddy making it every morning especially for me
Poured into a silver thermos Black deal
Sealed at the top as a mug
Daddy made the tea especially for me
Savoring it down my throat gave me safety cause daddy made the rooted tea
just for me
giving me powers to be

More freely cause daddy made the tea and simmered it well for me Early
morning at 5 a.m.

Daddy tea was soul love it was his bare black hands creating a meal of love
to nurture me
Daddy made tea from the root and woods of the tree planted from the soil
of rooted grandpa magical remedies of Gullah Carolinian Dust

Daddy no longer with me
One night at Calvary
As I slept over night by his bedside
As he died on his back looking straight through me

The tea now simmered with aromas sliding down my cheek

SISTER VINCENT

Fashion in 1976 for Me
For Star was two Pigtails
Perfectly, tightly parted down the middle
It was my green plaid jumper
With my slip starched iron
And the pigtails so perfectly tight
It made the shape of my almond eyes look
Even More Slanted
My Peter Pan collar was bleached white Ironed like I was about to go to
military school, instead of First Grade, Sister Vincent 101 First Grade Class
She was a deep pretty chocolate
Rectangular face woman
Reminded me of the German Chocolate
Cake my grandma Carolina baked last
Fall for my 5th Birthday
Looking at her skin
Made me want to bite deep into her
And receive the deep tingling sensations
On my tongue as when I licked the chocolate
Frosting from the bowl

Sister Vincent stood at the door well
With those skinny, bony, lanky legs,
In her blue and white habit…
She wore that habit as though she was making
A fashion statement for all black women
That they could even look good holding a yardstick,
Wearing a sterling silver chain with the crucifix around their neck,
With a blue polyester dress signifying a deep chocolate beauty
That I wanted to taste!

Even her shoes were black and ugly, but she stood on them like a black
queen statue

Ready to empower us with her look, experiences
And that yardstick against my little muscular legs
Of only 50 pounds
She started to look like a bodacious blackness
Ready to tear our buttocks up if we half step
When my Mama started to let my hand go
Sister Vincent fashion statement took on a new form,

A Giant, A Beast of a

NO-NONSENSE

WOMAN!

BASTARD CHILD

How fast he was in skill
He hammered, cleaned,
Fixed, farmed,
picked cotton,
Soiled the earth
Milked the cows

While others was thinking about it
Elijah had the job done
Older men put him in their circle to work

No older than 12

He defined
          Refined
Manhood
    With sweat and pride
In his boy stride
But
    Every Evening
He had to pass
A certain porch

Sat
    Big fat black
Woman
      Eating
Lots of greasy
                    Fat back

Throwing rocks at the
Cows as they walked
Pass

Throwing words of
"Bastard Child"
As Elijah briskly stride
In pride
Contributing to Mama

Burning fire shot
Through his blood

Passing Big Fat Black Woman

Eating lots of greasy fat back
Throwing rocks at the cows
As they walked Pass

Throwing words of
"Bastard Child"
As Elijah briskly
Stride   In   Pride

Tired of her
Nastiness to his pride
His young boy stride

Disgracing his Mama
Debasing his race

   Responding back
Throwing back
The words to her face

"Yeah I may be a Bastard Child
     But I ain't   no   white   man's child

At least My Mama stayed with her own kind
   You   just   roll   that   in your mind

I maybe a bastard child
But at least My Mama
Didn't have no half breed 'chillin'
With white men who have
Nuttin to do with them
Or   YOU

At least My Mama didn't sneak around
With white men on the riverbanks

        Creeping   on   creek banks

Big Fat Black Woman
Put hands on her hips

" You a sassy, sassy bastard!"

"And you   bought it
On   Fasty Assy!

What so sassy?
I'm passing by
On the public
Dust road
   Stop **talkin hind** my

Mama's back

While
Sit back eating
Your fat back
                Minding my Mama's back

You **'gotta enuf'** to do
Try cleaning up your shit

Sleeping by the creek
Dipping his snuff
Taking his stuff
The white man "Cum"

     Savagely Leaving
Creeping at night

Delivering   a white man child
               To   Your   Black   Husband

AINT RIGHT

Sassy SASSY Bastard

     Nasty,   NASTY   woman

Now you a disgrace
To the Black Man Race

 He now fuckin force
To face down while **lookin** up to white man
Bowed Down

Cause everybody look at this child
LOOK AT HIM
HE DIFFERENT
Hair
Color
Of Little Boy Assberry Beatter

He may be a "ASSberry"

But he sure ain't no kinfolks to the Beatter folks

No Mam
Now you take that

And
Leaved this Bastard Child Alone

Meddling in my Mama's Back!!!!!

SUICIDE 14

Didn't know it was going to happen
Getting off The 5 train at 7:00 am
Monday morning from East 59th street
       With Ivy and the crew.
Stopping at our spot
the famous
Dunkin Donuts
A call from the Valley boys to her beeper to stop by
Mario's House
Cut school and have a party
She was the left brain in the group
All eyes were on her to make the decision
"Like naw we gotta hit first period class
We must go to school!"
But Everyone is waiting for her to change her mind
She like ,
"nah no!"
They beg.
They wait as though she is the CEO of the pack.

As though she is the executive leader of the executive branch
As though she is the President and the Congress
Anticipating for her to change the order.

She gives in

The only problem is, she was never made for cutting.
Had E been with them who,
was an expertise in knowing how to
Call their private school and impersonate each of their parents
Stating they were under the weather, will not be in attendance
Remember this was the early 80's 1983 to be exact no cells no emails no
tracking devices no caller ID
But E was not with us that day.
She had taken the later train

Star knew she was not made for that

Stealing

24

the letter head from the school secretary and signing the principal name

Star was too serious for that
'cause for one
Her house was made up of an extended family
Grandma,   the housekeeper,   her dad- who worked
nights
& mother who stayed home

All they had to do was pass the school during the day and just by chance
 see school was in session
Her daddy, who beat her only once after she said,
"I wish you and mama was dead."
He tore her ass up with that old ripped up slave leather, raggedy belt
with the big buckle

She also never wanted to disappoint her parents or her self
But that crisp cool fall day in October all eyes were on her to make the
decision

"Ok what the hell let's do it."
VALLEY TRAIN NUMBER 5, BAYCHESTER AVE HERE WE COME

Kentlely was there;
          Mario her first boyfriend, *she'd eventually lose her cherry to* in his house
Ivy got the notion to call her mother
PLAYING IT OFF
as though she
WAS AT LUNCH AT OUR PRIVATE HIGH SCHOOL:

Mom's response was sharp.
"WHERE ARE YOU?
The SCHOOL has NOTIFIED ME and ALL of the PARENTS that
you are hanging with. . ."
BUSTED!!!

SHE BECAME FROZEN
THE LONGEST WALK HOME FROM THE VALLEY TO OUR
HOMES
WOULD WE GET THE BLACK SOUTHERN AND PUERTO RICAN
BEAT DOWN?

The SCHOOL has NOTIFIED ME and ALL of the PARENTS that
you are hanging with. . ."

BUSTED!!!

SHE BECAME FROZEN
THE LONGEST WALK HOME FROM THE VALLEY TO OUR
HOMES
WOULD WE GET THE BLACK SOUTHERN AND PUERTO RICAN
BEAT DOWN?

She heard her uncle with her father downstairs saying:
I BET SHE WAS THE LEADER OF THE PACT
Him gossiping edging her daddy on

It Was Like Fucking Jury Season, Or Lynch Mob! *Star thought*

Mom Came Home 5 Hours Later
Came Upstairs To Star Bedroom
Looked At Her
And Said :
"I AM SO DISAPPOINTED IN YOU."
then her mom began to cry.

DAMN! *Star thought it would have been better if she*

WHIPPED THE BLACK OFF HER ASS
OR
LYNCHED HER LIKE A SLAVE

Star began to **INFUSE** all the feelings of **RAPE & MOLESTATION** of
her **UNSPOKEN PAST**
                          Went Into Her Father's Armor,
& Took Every Pill She Saw

Willie Mae, next door, found Star in the room.

She woke up in Misericordia Hospital
she never received counseling-

**'CAUSE BLACK PEOPLE DON'T NEED NO THERAPIST, ALL
IN THEIR BUSINESS- WE GOT JESUS!**
All she remembered was the apple juice

The next couple of days
Visitors came with hugs
They said they loved her
& it was never

     discussed again!

She returned to her Park Avenue Private School
As the TOP honor roll student
          TOP model
TOP performer artist
never for it to be discussed.
SHE DANCED
CHOREOGRAPHED the PAIN
                    & BECAME

CONGENIAL
SERIOUSLY
     FOCUSED

Cut off her first boyfriend.
HE WAS TOO YOUNG
IMMATURE
&
JUST NOT WORTHY OF HER.

*Never knowing that all the ugly & invasion of her body
would catch up later in her 20's*

BUT MAMA
     DADDY
        AUNTIE
          & UNCLES
DID WHAT THEY KNEW BEST! (*at the time*)
LOVED
SUPPORTED
HUGGED
ADORED
PRAYED
&
SUPPORTED
ALL HER DREAMS
From Education to Professional Dreams!

THE UGLY

THE RAPE
THE MOLESTATION

                                                    WAS

NEVER SPOKEN OF
until
HER 22-YEAR-OLD BREAKDOWN.

28

AS HE DROVE ME

Every morning
He knew
He felt my
Blues
Saw the salt
Leave my body
Fixed my over easy eggs on white bread
Melted American grilled cheese
With Hellman's Mayo
Enjoying the yellow yoke gush out on the soft white bread
with a thin slice of southern ham
Peppermint hot tea. -*His gifted retired magical thermos hands*

As we drove across the Grand Concourse
He said

" Look baby girl any man would want you. I would want a woman like you.
You're educated driven beautiful; always stepping pushing reaching for
more never settling but reaching and even pushing your man.

You are making good money so don't fear. Don't Fret.

Use what is already in your hand, you haven't realized what you have
accomplished in such a short life time.

There are many others who are empty, lost and broken.
Stop being unfulfilled.
You are a young viable woman
And you telling me your husband told you
Sex- is only for procreation so he will be preserving his sperm- THAT IS
SOME BULLSHIT
A husband should be doing it full time and pleasing his wife
So when he doesn't touch you saying some fucking dumb twisted
backwards abnormal shit like 'sex is only for
procreation'- IT AIN'T FUCKING NORMAL!

Do what you gotta do
look at me good
do what you gotta do
whatever that is
you hear?
To please and fulfill what is in here"

He touched my heart as he spoke.

I looked out the window as cabs school buses city buses passed and teared up except, no tears could fall, it melted inside and made me throw up.

"Now I love who you love. If you love a gorilla, I love a gorilla. But when you stop loving the gorilla I will too.

It destroys a part of me to see you lifeless
If I can fix it let me know

But that is some unnatural bullshit with you being sexually Neglected in lieu of
His ???
Then when he said, He got raped by that girl
Who he had in his bed- I thought I heard everything.

Baby do what you gotta to do to make you feel what you need to feel to be all woman black woman again.
I got you baby girl
Daddy got you
I'm holding you up…!!!"

THE TONGUE

It cuts
It locks
It Licks
It inspires
It cuts
It makes love
It starts wars
It kills spirit
It cuts
It can curse you
It can taste you
It can hurt you
It can love you
The first kiss
It's French
I don't know why
'cause
He was Black American
With a thin long pink tongue
Wearing adidas sneakers
Skin brown bronze greased up
But that tongue
It spoke no French
Yet gave a funny feeling in my stomach left & moist panties

The tongue was a snapping space
With cussing contest
and Mama jokes that could go to 100 with a fight or a laugh
Right or Left
Your Mama So This
Your Mama So That
Sometimes the tongue made you laugh until you cried
or wanted to pee on yourself
Other times
It made you sad that you wanted to hide under a rock and cry yourself to
sleep
'Cause
Words *like*
"You so black night time can't see you"
"You're so light, ivory soap is like your twin"
or
"You're so bright you're like a light"

"You're ugly and black, even Aunt Jemima disowned you
"nobody wants you…
you ain't shit……
you will never be nuttin
You just like your trifling daddy or cracked mama"

That Tongue Did A Lot Of Things And It Sure Had Nothing To Do With
French In The Hood.

Relationships

TRANSFORMATION
DEFORMATION
PROCLAMATION

Turning into Something
　　She no longer knew
Some say it was growth
　　She thought it was part of her hell

As a woman
　　A black mule

She thought she was supposed to go through it alone
Ashamed to reveal the illness of her thoughts
The Scars left on the mind
She was supposed to bare it
Transform Into A New Being Of A Proclaimed Strength
How in the hell could she transform?
When her insides became
Deformed
[Mutilated]
Her appearance was clueless to everyone
But her soul
Maybe it wasn't so bad stepping outside of self
Taking on the demons that entered her essence
Toured at her beauty
Assassinated her talents
Entering her essence
Yeah
She was a black woman with invisible scars
That only spoke to her mind
Proclamation of revealing her caged hell with her man was impossible

　　He could not hear her cries
　　　　See her scars
Touch her deformed body
　　Cause he

Was too absorbed in a Sickness OF HIS OWN

INFATUATION

I cannot be any man's fantasy,
Victim of an
    Infatuation, or his childhood broken dreams

No baby girl, Not I!
    Sleeping with a dreamer, a murderer, a rapist, a molester
Of your beauty, your total existence, is deadly to the soul

Naw Baby Girl!
    Naw! No

I have to be his Queen and He King
We have to be equals when it comes to our love,
    Our life,
 Our babies.   You doll face.   I mean baby girl

Our lovemaking must taste like sweet deep rich chocolate
      Sometimes a creamy solid white
But always fulfilling to the Spirit.
    Yes the Essence.

My man can't be just a Candy man Licker
    You know what I mean baby girl
Nor a minute man
    I damn sure can't be his hooker, his hoe or should I
Say "Whore" like they do downtown.

  Baby girl, doll face
      Nor can the nigger be mi pimp
 Nor shrimp

    You know the type:

{Them got damn short men, tall men, black men, rich men, poor men, white men, mixed men, confused men, and all inbreed with the ingredients of INSECURITY}

You know the type:

Now Baby girl you talking about sleeping with Hitler, Machismo Misogynist at its lowest ghetto point

A Midget, fidget complex, sinking drowning your insides in

A mess, Now you got a man made up of a fucking collage
You got fragmentations
Altercations
Reparations

Now you have layers of issues and different masks entering you
Trying to smother/overpower your creativity, your nakedness

Naw girlfriend. You don't want no NIGHTMARE

   Time to Take Inventory
Reassess , Retake
   Review and RENEW YOU
I need a Potato
   Steak filet mignon, or whatever holds his stomach, Variety, Diversity,
Reality……. If I get Micky Dee's it should suffice,

He needs to be a Simplistic
Artistic
     Hard
          Soft
               Gentle
Non-toxic
     Freaky kind of good smelling Funk
That allows you to cream
          Dream
Exasperate
 With
Organic
  Multiple
Tantalizing
     Sensations
Running through my thighs
 Tormenting my spirit and
Dancing into my soul
          RENAISSANCE MAN!
          NOW WESE A TALKING BABY GIRL

TASTELESS UNFELT

You no longer had the flavor scent
Stale swag
 was crippled
Touch impaired
Vision backwards

Laughter replaced with a crying river

No longer saturated with impeccable taste

Passion replaced with diluted EX
Complied with Grey intimacy

Routine swiftly changed from right to lose
 Unrecognizable deplorable between her thighs wrestling to her heart
fixated to memory

Fertilizer contaminated by the rotten eggs consuming the atmosphere
Hiding any stars to reach up to
Comfortless

Nothing could bring that warm lily rose lavender scent back into their
present or future
Too much flavorless staleness has ghost the rapture of past history
For
Resolutions Manifestations & Ramifications
Intertwined
Not knowing where to begin or end
No middle piece to fix
All broken pieces of she knows heartbreak

IN THE DELIVERY ROOM?

What Are Your Goals?
Where Do You See Yourself In The Next Five Years?

My baby boy at 4 reminded him," let's buy mommy a gift to take to her room for she and baby sister."

She just delivered an 8 pound 10 oz baby girl out her vagina with over 15 plus hours of labor pains;
His first real conversation is a 20/20 interview
Of
"WHERE DO YOU SEE YOURSELF IN FIVE YEARS?"

This nigger has become
"The Miseducated Negro" of them all.

-Wait let's switch off for a moment

It was just 6 years ago when they met.
She, 21, straight out of undergrad
By spring semester, She, 22, in grad school focusing on pursuing education with a long-term focus of JD/PHD.
Then marriage house baby boy came along.
With detours of growth and messy in a young marriage.
He's not college educated
BUT like a black woman,
She, his personal educational life coach
Outlined & helped him finally move up in rank in the Navy from E5 to E6

(Ladies why do we do that?)
Coached,
Cheered,
Typed College papers,
Even had her mother getting his transcripts and even let him use her family for highest homeland security clearance recommendations because they pulled weight.

So no this Negro did not *JUST* step foot in her space and asked his wife although he was already creeping and sucking another tit-
after almost choking her to death earlier in her pregnancy

SO HE ASKED HER WHAT HER 5 YEAR PLAN WAS??
Honestly She wanted to say,

"to stay on my knees Mastah as I continue to
please, obey, and abide.
Her Words couldn't come out
She lost her voice 'cause
Her insides were beaten into a non-fertilization moisture turned inside out.

DID THIS MOTHER FUCKER JUST ASK HER WHAT HER 5 YEAR PLAN WAS?

Her response should have been like this:

> 1.Get my pussy repaired for the next nigger who knows it's worth
> 2.Get surgery on my heart because it is in cardiac arrest
> 3.Have the GyN remove the keloids from giving natural birth
> 4.Get as far the fuck away from you never to look back

AND

> 5.Retreat to therapy and God in order to find me again so I'm able to detect ASAP a miseducated Negro like you

That is what he would have loved for her to say to justify his already guilty agenda
He to move up with a come up with a clean-up woman who he thought could make him look better by hiding his secret scars

GREEN EYED MONSTER

Green eye monster liberated the fears of a sex revolution between the
cheeks and v spot
Of my thighs and extended legs
With one breast deformed
and the other almost gone
he never looked at them
But through me
I never knew
Nor Phantom the mystic
of how the green eyes made love
to my mind
Spirit
Soul
& Backside

Even without a touch
Every organic organism on my body
A deep black intimacy of articulation
Never knew to feel so deep black green and blue
Unimaginative in my burnout
Vulnerability of chemo
By a man
A real man
A hustling man
A handy man
An engineer of a man
Navigated my womanhood between the sheets
& above the earth
It was a secret sacred space exclusively for me
It made me cry through multiple orgasms even when we sat and wrote love
letters of affirmations to each other in bed
It was too good a juicy good a fulfilled wet moist good

Cause my love for green eyed monster was one that was on the edge
making love on the
rooftop elevator penthouse
Beach house

While embracing my now deformed body of uneven Stripes
Reconstructed breasts
with the **Renaissance Revival Sensations**
Called

Sexual healing

When our monsters of our dreams
Converted into a man;
A real man
A handyman

Who *was* Trained Well

In how to use
His hands
& heart
to heal me.

MAKE UP SEX

Is like a jazz blues
R&B Tune.

A smooth
                                soft

provocative melody.
Entering you
with a
Hip Hop Beat

        Holding you tightly
LICKING
&

                                    SUCKING
                                          the saxophone

into you.
Softly
                         Soulfully

Deeply feeling
                                            a Black Afro Rhythm

SLIDE
    Into your hips
with fingers tapping
   on your black keys
 As your back
Unfolds
Into a frozen arched dancer.
        Leaning   way
               -    way   back
Into a v-spot position
Mesmerizing
                        Stimulating
Hormones
Of laughter.
        Sunshine, is
that
Erected Light

THUNDER

                Into your legs & arms
        Flexing
and
                                        Pointing
Into a whirlwind of
Fire
            And
                        Water
Contractions
Released
Extension
                                        Pelvic
                        Torso
Moving Experiences

Music Plays So Loud
 In Your Heart
                                                        &
Spirit
As the connection
To the drums enters your soul
with
            Multiple Vibrations
of orgasms.

Wrapped into the arms of a CEO
 Savvy

            Tech
 Musician
Artist
                                            Expertise

Connoisseur
of
HER   Body   Mind   Spirit

Magically
UNFOLDING
                        Uncontrollable
 Layers of mask

Shedding   to
Disappear
    &&
Evaporate
Into SHE

                              hole of

A
   V-Spot
of

Her Birth Canal
BUT FIRST
Connecting
IN SYNC   THEIR
ALPHA
Soulful Physical
with a
smooth loud
POETIC LYRICAL
Jill Scott
Acapella Beat
PUSHING
FORTH like a
Strong Silent Song
   called
I'm Every Woman"

SHE
 submitting herself to him
in order to make he feel
NOOOO
MORE BLUES
But,
       Exclusively NEGOTIATED
Jazz Rhythms
Created a whole new melody
that night
of
MAKEUPSEX
No Strings Attached.

Except those Rhythms between their Skin
        that Exchanged Untamed Energy
said A Whole Lot
Filling
Both
Them
Up
Left Voiceless
& that
DRUNKEN Love
 Without
      Singing   any lyrics
JUST *music*
 Felt in
their nakedness
& touch
As
      He N She
         Lay in rapture of each other's song
         Into the dawn
         Shining stars
         Of a full moon!

371 BROKE

"Where do I begin?
Oh now I remember…..
The day the Family Court Judge said
"Temporary Child support will be $900.00 for two."
Then husband denied the unborn girl as his
"Yes, darling don't be surprised. What a MF will do, especially a man, a
black Puerto Rican angry, short, insecure man…"
Yes. I know what you are thinking:
Divorce the wife,
but never the children
Always Respect the wife
and
Mother of your children
Even if you could not by any means keep your penis in check
CHECK MATE!

Now hush, let me finish telling you this narrative, farce
We know it was his wife
Whose belly was falling
Carrying
Filled Up Heavily

HEAVENLY

His Actions were layered with musk and another pussy
Confirmed the night he choked and squeezed the stitches from her mouth
Gushing blood shooting to ceiling
Gasping for air.
Scratching his face,
Pinned down to bed, *their baby boy son jumps on his daddy's back*
His Power Ranger sword
" GET OFF MY MOMMY!"

Military base - choked wolves worked

Reflecting on Thanksgiving of that year when she called all excited to say,

"We are having another baby, I'm pregnant! "
His telephone response, being her husband and all

"THAT IS THE LAST THING I NEED TO HEAR"

-"Is that what I think he said" she thinks, *"That is the last thing I need to hear"*

Her quick black girl Harlem comeback
"NO WORRIES, IT AIN'T YOURS ANYWAY IT IS THE IMMACULATE CONCEPTION LIKE MARY WITH JESUS."
Playing back and rolling back in her mind the eagerness for him to stick it in raw Election Day begging for another baby
371
So draining
Then in court
After Mass
In order to dodge the pay
Says to Judge
"THIS FETUS IS NOT MINE"
In order to dodge & prolong not paying child support for 2
Forced to financially contribute to the baby boy
When baby girl was born that hot Virginia Beach Summer at their home in Hampton, VA

Wife was forced to drive 400 miles to DC court
To get baby girls mouth swabbed
She held her on her hip next to her tit
 Silently crying invisible blood, fighting tears ,

Next court hearing - defense mechanism
He dropped out of Navy to avoid taking care of
Baby girl
NYC Puerto Rican Female DC Family Court Judge
Said *" Sorry sir you are voluntarily unemployed. had a job and voluntarily left it. You're still obligated by law and forced to pay $900 and 12 months retro child support pay,"*
Calculated that in my mind, that's $10,800
Girrrrllll…..
He looked across the court
Pointed his hand at wife and said

"YOU'RE A DEAD BLACK BITCH!"

Judge said," Repeat that, what did you say?"
This Nigger began swinging
4 Court officers took him out with each arm and leg in hand. With him kicking and cursing the whole time.
His clean up mistress
Represented him in court
To help release him

Resulted in him later paying only

3 7 1 for two babies
Cause he went into the civilian world to hide his money then
Snuck back into Navy
With a court order still at 371, now to be changed
Wife too tired 'cause now
Breast Cancer attacked her body
Father just died of Pancreatic Cancer
All she knew was to fight smart and hire
A NY Savvy Lawyer to arrive in DC and shut it down!!!
 She won a custody case, won her house that he abandoned,
and her parents paid the mortgage while she was left pregnant and barefoot

With 371
For the remainder of her babies' years from toddlers to teens to college

Total called 371
Called not child support
But
a
non support
371
Broke
but
not
Broken!!!

STOP!

When I stop texting my thoughts of inspiration
or sharing special moments of events
 Happening By
GIVING YOU
A GLIMPSE
OF ME,

My reality that is more to than what the eye can see,
it is more than my swag
Persona
 or class of elevation
or scent of fragrance
            or the way
I OWN A ROOM
With confidence
                              but so many layers of me
vulnerable street brightness
with Strings of darkness

                                        that gives weight to my

past
 But
           cannot stifle my present.
She craves to be in your rotated rapture
 but with her
Rowing the tides
to tell her unmasked
latte mocha cinnamon race of taste

                                   pitying the salt years of tears

that resurfaced a hell of darkness
 in her   loneliness
REFLECTIVE of
PRESENT
STRUGGLES

HIJACK PUNK

Stop riding me on empty
Dry rot empty
Can't lubricate
Empty
No orgasm empty
Heartless
This is for me
This is my stuff
My ride
My journey
By invitation only
Who gave you entitlement?
To enter yourself
Into me
Into my dreams
Into my head
Into my heart
YOU CANNOT TAKE WHAT IS NOT YOURS!

Cause when you grab push punch choke-
Then Runaway
you just
A BITCH
With a penis

NBA TRICK

Playing basketball
Dribble dribble swish
Playing basketball

Trying to catch the ball
Yes becky with the so called good hair was trying to catch the ball

Not the orange leather black one

But long black thick one
Dribble
Dribble
SWISH!

As she shaked her hips
Wiggled Her Tits
Licked Her Lips

Dribble
Dribble
SWISH!

His black goddess sat in the bleachers shining and cheering him on like the
star she is.
Tall,
Lean,
Curvaceous,
Clapping,
Screaming,
Praying, &
Crossing her fingers
While Becky,
Bent down under his legs in a split
Bobbing her head trying to catch the ball
The black ball

LOVE GLANCE

Maybe it was a glance
Maybe it was a deep conversion
Maybe it was a dream
Maybe it was just not enough
Maybe it was not long enough
Maybe it was a glance ending to
Second new beginnings
Maybe it was a regret
Too much thinking
Cause he told her what it is
Women want the trust
Truth but fantasize on how it should be
This feeling took her way back
Flashback
old feelings of numbness watered down with dumbness
It was May 1991 her college graduation from Barnard
He said let's leave the graduation celebration at her house
and go to the park
Need to talk
and be alone he said
It was her graduation day
so much had happened between them
rejection of who he could no longer be inside or outside of her
She knew the capabilities of his tongue
his tongue was death
or the way he washed her hair
Cooked her food
oiled her down
Then wrapped her up
could not fix this thing he was trying to tell her
he sat her on the park bench
Took out the vile
and said this is my mistress
what is that a fucking Jennie bottle
naw it is crack
He wanted to put all the cards on the table
She thought this was no longer her problem
She ran
took her heels off and kept running
he kept calling after her
a ghost had broken her
She fell Into the grass

thanking the Gods that two months ago she eradicated the deadness he put inside her belly she knew and thanked the Gods and the Ancestors that she did not give birth to a black crack baby who had to be sacrificed in order for both of them

to dismiss their high school College sweetheart journey

She ran right into marriage with a different king of ghost that became her monster

So She now understands to protect the invitation of another to her sacred unveiling space

DEAR MR. GOODBAR

Please it
Isn't scary
Isn't good
Isn't scary
Falling deeply into
A milk chocolate hole
Filled with nuts
Not any nuts
But your nuts
Nuts filled with
Wishing
Fulfillment
Vision
History
Patience
Kindness
Gentleness
A black deep chocolate hole that the nuts
Fear to overcompensate the solidness of the bar and its expectations
Not understanding
The chocolate hole doesn't alpha the nuts but make it a solid complete
rectangular bar ready to eat every which way
Satisfying the insatiable appetite
Of soulfulness called no conditions
But an infinitive love of intuitiveness
Discernment overpowered by the chocolate hole which consumes the nuts
but not any nuts only his nuts completely compacted into a fetus position
of his soft strong nutted Brown canvass arms
Alpha and Omega knew that night in which the chocolate hole was filled
with his exclusive nuts a black power couple was born out of love

HIPS

HIP CON-nection

Pushing through
                            that bone
A wall of
PAIN
   Unbearable   Yearning
for his
Wild
                                    WIDE
Big
  Brown
     Hands
to
        Gently
           TOUCH
           TAP
             MASSAGE
  Lay
      Hard
        &&
         Soft
As he poured
The Boiling HOT
Coconut oil
onto Her.
As it splashes
           Her hip
                Tasting
Her Back
 Slip
Sliding it all   around.
Back n Forth
Forth n Back
            onto Her

Inner - Outer
Firm
Dance

THIGHS
Wild
WIDE
Big Brown Hands
 Gripping
Her inner being
yearning like her cat.
Ebony in heat
UNBEARABLE *wiggle*

                                        Bump

Hustle
As *His Hands*
                    Rubbed
Her
 Soulfully
      Ethnically
Rhythmically
like **CONGA DRUMS**
 Resonating
Jumping

                                        Pushing

Her Torso

 into a Trance
She slowly
RISES UP
like the   **Nubian Egyptian Belly Dancer**
Squirming
on Her stomach
Rolling slippery on her back

 Extending Her Arms into the Air
to pull up

While bopping
Rolling
             Gyrating
                              Her Way Up   *onto the*
Pillow
of the Bed
 To Become

                         His
Exclusive
Private Dancer
with Coconut Oiled on Head
DRIPPING
            SHINING
To Her
                    Behind
Thigh
Ass
Neck
                    Arm
V-Spot
                                    & Chess Walls
            Extending
Her Leg
into a
Pirouette
                then
Passé
  Falling into a Split onto Him
                                                In Him
Inside
Every Fiber
 of
  Him

FEVER

Giving me fever not the kind that makes you hot cold sweaty weak the kind that makes you weep not a weep that makes you cry but more like a sigh of love making really good love making yes that is what that fever was like a good weeping diving into a sweet soft hard loving the kind that makes you create; it makes you choreograph timeless heartfelt heartbroken heart melted heart revived kind of movements; yes giving me fever to push forth through extended arms contracting to a silhouette and no glass or beer cans or burnt offerings or fake laughter or broken images or torn panties or recycled love to break; or deter me Cause this fever it is inclusively designed for every fragment, every dissected and broken body; don't let the good looks fool you or the messy hair distract you cause a new horizon is here; it ain't coming it has arrived!!!!

Bold Black Beautiful Dramatic Ecstatic Not diluted Fearless Fierce Kind of Fever!!!

Why Again?

TIRED

So
Sorry
for not
Being Sorry
So
Sorry
for not
Being Available
So
Sorry
for
Being me
--------I don't think So
'Cause
if
I *was*
SORRY for that
 I WOULD BE.
SORRY!!!

EXPERIMENT

It was a chemistry and biology experiment
Plugging two opposites but almost similar can get a chemical explosion
Really wish initially the experiment was set up like a trick then could delete
any chemistry and just be biological physical
No intellectual conversation which promotes emotional biological and
chemistry energy

She really wishes she could change everything
But then the chemistry of tears sporadically rolling down her cheek
unmasking the true vulnerability of it all
Still figuring out why
No closure
Over a phone
An instrument separating dialogue but same time expressing heartfelt
feelings
The word CHOKE
Let it go!

CARDIAC ARREST

Next week into last week
Not knowing this week, he would arrest me
Coming into my house
Opening me up to his grounded old savory savvy humorous old school
swag

Never knew he could open up my window pains and make it feel like a
cardiac arrest
No not the
one that makes you die
but gives your life a
Resurrected
Tantalizing
                              Breathing
Running
Through My Veins
Kneeling, Sighing, even to the point of tearing
not sure if I suppose to be exonerated from my fears
with walls now shattering &
Legs extending to be gently entered into
While using his tongue to
Widen My Hips
 Back Arched
Toes pushed into a relieve
'cause he rocked the hell out that house last night
 My cardiac arrest has been healed
with his touch,
                    a caring humanness *TOUCH.*

*I know this new resurrected crucifixion of a cardiac cross erection is a sweaty moist
scented lavender oil man scent of Red Jamaican Rum
It has me open to a different arena of a sacred space
the kind a woman like me should have resonating through
my mind*
Erecting My Thighs
Penetrating My V Spot

All with an arrest of a new resurrected heartfelt destress
Simplified drama free flowing kind of cardiac arrest

Black Breast

CHEMO AFFIRMATIONS

Must tell it now.
Every morning bald headed
Dressed Up
                    And
 All
 Would get up in the morning
 Put my lipstick and eyeshadow on
 With long earrings
 Or
 Sometimes just a ball cap
or
 Kente Cloth wrap
 And
Drop my babies off to school.
 That was the first battle.
My baby girl was in Universal Pre-K
And
My first-born son was in third grade.
I jumped in my brand-new black Acura
And blasted the words ***Never Give Up*** from the speakers to the vibrations
of my mind.
Hanging on to **Every Word** as
It overflowed
To a different kind
Of
Breast less

HOLIDAY CANCER

After 9/11 and the year my dad died of Pancreatic Cancer. That summer my babies were taken away to DC with no address. Didn't know that after 9/11 my body would be terrorized after Thanksgiving. In the summer I sat on the porch steps in front of my house and felt a burning sensation in my left breast. It went away, or I went away in my thoughts to another place. Then it was the beginning of November and I just finished teaching my last period dance class to my 8th grade students at MS 113. I had a prep period and my inner voice came so hard over me and said," Go to the doctor now. Something isn't right." My breast had a knot and burning sensation. I went to my Principal's office and shared with her that I need to leave and go to my Gynecologist, since I had a free last period mayI be excused. She too was a breast cancer survivor. She was like, "Leave go now!" When I arrived at Dr. K's office he was like, "No worries it is probably nothing." A man doctor telling a woman not to worry about her pain. I needed a referral for the mammogram. He told me it would probably take a long time in months or weeks before I was seen. His voice became noise in my head. I pulled out my cell phone sitting on the GYN table with my gown on still undressed. The lady on the other line said, "Mam someone just cancelled and if you can get over to the office right now, you can get the mammogram." I jumped in my car and was able to make the appointment that day. It was a painful squeeze, but I left every worry or concern at that office afterwards.

Thanksgiving came, and my babies would be in DC visiting their father. I spent Thanksgiving with my Cousin in Stamford Connecticut. When I got home, my mother told me I had an appointment with the oncologist about my results regarding my mammogram. She didn't want to spoil my Thanksgiving, so she didn't tell me. Sitting in front of the oncologist he said, "We discovered a mass on the left side of your breast and it is Stage 4 Cancer." Those were words of death to my ears. All I could do was cry and scream hysterically and think of my young babies 4 and 8. My mother walked me out of the corridor of the hospital holding my hand. She whispered in my ear, "You will get through this you are strong." Mama voice healed me. Those words slapped me into faith. I believed it....

My mother found a top Breast Surgeon, Dr. S, to get a second opinion. She made me feel safe, protective, and so good about myself. She gave me a biopsy to confirm what was seen from the mammogram. Christmas Eve I had a lumpectomy. Dr. S came to my bed the next day to let me know they found cancer in the lymph nodes and she wanted me to come to her office to discuss alternatives after I get out of hospital. I cried again. But this time Silent tears came down. It was just she and I in the hospital room.

She recommended that I get a mastectomy and reconstruction of my breast during one surgery. When I wake up from the surgery my breast would be removed but reconstructed with the fat from my stomach and tattooed nibbles. Psychologically it felt as though I never got a breast removed the first time.

On Valentine's Day it was a 12 hour or more surgery of a double mastectomy; Followed by 6 months of chemo. On Palm Sunday all my hair fell out.

I learned to follow my spirit and faith. My first cancer journey was followed by Holidays. Thanksgiving cancer was discovered, Christmas Eve lumpectomy, Valentine's Day mastectomy and Palm Sunday chemo hair loss bald

Did I forget to mention the arrest after the surgery?
Or the death of my Pastor a few months later
Or when I began teaching at the college
Or the end of my custody battle going back and forth to DC
Or traveling across NY area from upstate in the cold to my son's football games
Or my daughter scoring the highest in nation in math/reading and being honored at Sarah Lawrence College at 9 years old by John Hopkins University Center for Talented Youth
Or being awarded Parent of the year at my son's 5th Grade School, graduation and see him get several awards and valedictorian;
And the house almost burned down with my first born inside while in HS During the Era of My Holiday Cancer????

CANCER FOLLOW UP REPEAT

1/19/18 - I was at my favorite doctor's office visit with Dr. Shapiro. She is my breast surgeon who removed the cancer three times. She always reminds me of our first meet 17 years ago coming into her office lean, flowing, and erected like a dancer. She reminds me how stunning my presence was and how skinny I was then. Ironically during that first battle with Cancer I was told by a specialist you are beautiful. Did not really know my strength then like I know it now. My babies were young, and Dr. Shapiro had teenagers. She is now a grandmother with a son who is a lawyer. What I remember about her first encounter was the advocacy kick ass attitude she had for me. The labs had taken awhile which mixed up my report. She went all in, then they appeared immediately. Then at the time her husband was editor for the Arts section of New York Times. As an artist myself, I felt I was with the baddest, brilliant, bohemian, artistic, and anointed doctor. We always had our shared conversations in her office giving me portraits of life. I recall the time I brought my children to see her, so she could make them feel reassured that they too didn't have breast cancer. My son was in 5th grade and daughter in kindergarten at the time.

 My last visit that summer where my skin on the side in which the Cancer was removed became dark, peeling, raw, and red. She and my oncologist collaborated with the urgency of energy. Once the results came back negative, she shared, "I feel so responsible for your life. You are special to me." Maybe she makes everyone feel that way, but it was what I needed to hear. It gave me new wings.

READY OR NOT READY?!

The noise inside gets full of nothingness
Stagnant Fearful Hyped on Darkness.

Why is it that the world has opened up even when things tried to smother
me with their hysteria?
Two additional children
Not by birth canal *but*
Life Canal *were*
Born *into* my Life Canal
Compelled to help Save someone else from Pain.
Has Caused me a Roller Coaster of
JOY   PAIN   CHALLENGES

Fixated volunteered to Shackles
A Prison Sentence of an Entire Family Unit.

Scene I
Cancer was not enough
Breast removed with was not enough;
Seeing my children
my babies Rise into Brilliance
Thinking yes!
 "I Can Do the Same
With **My Life Canal Circumstances**
Got This…."
 Some things You Can Not Do
But Only Let Go

Revolution Evolution

TO BE YOUNG AND GIFTED

Their movements voices music lyrics poetry film boldness
 To be to do
Gives me Fire.
                    Not knowing how my darkness brought into light

By publishing realizing the power of my voice resonating through the
breast,
thighs, minds, and bold behinds of female college dorm women in search
of their sacred space
To Be To Do
The other black ballerina bird song singer born, college black artist
organizing creative sacred space with no apologies;
The other black activist using her modern dance her voice through the
written word creating a Non-Profit to encourage social political
consciousness
To Be No Longer Impoverished or Invisible Because of Poverty Black
Talented and Young
To Be To Do
 The third he black dancer vulnerable
 in Alvin Ailey
to explore
 to be free
with his high kicks so fierce
 not ashamed to come to me and cry
To Be To Do
 To stay with me in his solitude dancing
 Through his pirouettes
 Executed Leaps.
 I love them All so Deeply
 Because they allowed me to mirror me
To Be To Do
Unapologetically Boldly Recognizing the Young Gifted Black me again
In the Dancing directing writing of a born again me.
I got so torn up in a story that almost killed me;
Hell, when your spirit becomes choked
You're not breathing anymore
 You're just on **Life Support**.

NEW MIRROR

New bras and new panties
Giving rebirth to her womanhood
Making her sexy resurrected at the dawn of the New-Year
Forgot how to switch across the floor in her heels
Flinging lipstick eyeshadow to bring out the lashes
The eyes with pride
She often glared at the reflection in the mirror with pride
Falling back in a love affair with herself
In an
Organic way
For so long
So easy so distracted
in the
Too stagnated routine
Of
Nurturing a nation, a tribe;
Sewing roots into everyone else soil;
Disregarding her own dirt;

Teaching coaching fixing repairing cheerleading
Cleaning their mess up
in order
for their come up;
Neglecting her inner beauty
Which illuminated
Her outer beauty
When did internal and external forces of beautification become a collage
lost in fragmentations?
Then there was a new mother with a newborn
Who was a millennial fashionista?
And now spends her days
Dressing and meeting the demands of her baby
Without ever taking the time
To really look in the mirror anymore!
New Bras and New Panties
good perfume lipstick and
a mirror to stop fixate redo
Has given both women
Their resurrected self-love affair ANEW
With a deep rich new fertilizer to strut and own into now Exclusively for
her!

Y AGAIN AND AGAIN!

As the trees brush and stroke my back I thank the creator for what it is. Whipped into submission without commission fixation within manifestation of destination journeying to an awakening of justification without a lynch mob or jury. Playing back the blues of determination met by segregation a wall built up to stop growth and spring up weeds without seeds.

Smoking grass without branches or trees but high off of the dust of climate change met by Wall Street in the middle of a slave block. Turning back the head of time being told my saneness does not relate to humanness

Cause I'm 1 third of a person without independence but forbearance

When policies are being made in DC they equate the same as when it was made by their forefathers that excluded the brown me the female me the reproductive me only to consume the white male privilege brother who DNA is so grated in 400 plus years of pre-civil war ideology of anti-emancipation but justification of incarceration by controlling the psychology of the mind playing on the psychic.

Change was evolving when the terrorists on her soil America USA created the atmosphere the tone the setting the characters that assassinated Kennedy, Dr. King Malcolm X Medgar Evers when we thought hope change has come with Barack they are rioting to tear it back into the rape darkness of a historical time when "America was Great Again" for only the few the White Supremacist the Haves who steal from the have nots.... The Exploiters who exploit the vulnerable so Again and Again the trees brush and stroke my back but this time I am dodging the nook hanging from it.

HATE BLACK BOYS

Disheartened as he chuckles
We stopped by state troopers coming and going
College tour trip just
he and I
My first-born son
His birth was the happiest and saddest day of my life
As I held him FOR THE FIRST TIME
I cried

Looked over to my husband THINKING

"Boy child black boy child
Grow up different than white boy child"

Grandma response FROM Southern roots replies:
"No worries him light skin; be treated more privilege"

All I thought Willie Lynch still got us in Mental Shackles
Skin tones, wide nose, thick lips, wooly hair, big hips, thick behind, plump
round and tall burly black, dark, or yellow black man in spaces with guns of
bullets and nooks to their head
Historical Mass Public Holocaust Lynchings of their genitals cut off and
testicles shoved into mouth hanging from trees has been replaced now with
brains blown away

Please spare me the white privilege myth
cause my black boy must be smarter,
 more articulate, and
intellectually armed
 Street smart wit with warfare born

When they stop and frisk him
They will not see his yellow skin or curly hair
Nigger Black to Make America Great Again
Will not see IVY League Graduate
Mechanical Engineering
Graduating top of class in his High School
Competing debating at Yale and Harvard through Frederick Douglass
Approach and National Robotic and Chess Tournaments
Damn you… They will only see a Black boy from a Harlem disregarding his
yellow black skin

Fixating on Making him a statistic
All Caught up in creating enough prisons based on how many 4th grade black boys fail
the New York State test
 Born out of a historical
white male master slave establishment
Designed to water down my boy
by drowning His Black Mind Spirit and body
with their white robes whips and burning crosses

Even though my first black born boy who was born a black African prince

Which was born to exceed the standards of a misconception
of their fears
rooted in a psychosis of narcissism
white patriarchal forefathers enslaved mentality

"You cannot have my Black boy
He ain't for sale lynching or police bullet killing

Cause God and I made a pact
Which resulted in him living pass his 24th Birthday to be a man a black man
a man who

 Uses chess to master navigate through their plan.

W.E.B Dubois quite often spoke of it as

The Double Consciousness of Black folks!"

FORSAKEN SELF

Asked Banker
WHAT DO YOU DO FOR KELLY?
"My **life is my children and family**."
But What do you do for you?!!!!!
"I do my children"
"I do my husband"
"I do my siblings"
"I DO MY BOSS"
"ANY WHICH WAYHE WILL COMMAND ME TO PLEASE THEM!!!"

But

"What makes you happy just for you?
What is that 10 percent
or even 1 percent you do everyday
out of the 100 percent for your tribe?"

She looked with no breath…
Color flushed
Skin became pale dark

Dismayed by the question
She sat
QUIETLY
ALMOST LIFELESS

SEARCHING for SOUL
  FOR clues
 answers
Reflecting
      Even
 Searching through Google
For
 The
 Answer

       While bleeding tears ran through her thighs

Paralyzed by a sharpening pain through her behind

Rampantly hijacking her abdomen

By racing
through her
BIRTH CANAL YES, HER birth canal!!!
She began to cry for the rocks mountains and clouds to hear
REACHING OUT TO THE MOON
  She fell into her knees
 Folded her hands in prayer
And
screamed out an EARTH-SHAKING SHATTERING SIGH

"**God why have I forsaken myself,**
 when clearly that was not a commandment…...?
Why but Why have I run away from me forsaking my innate being?"

DEATH GREETED ME BEFORE PALM SUNDAY INTO GOOD FRIDAY

No thank you
Death
It surrounded my car
In a jail cell
Black sparrows
With guns surrounded
My car
Ma Death greeted me
No thank you
It took records
Truth
Background check
Bloodline
History
And Facts
To release me from the shackles
As I stand in jail from
8 am till 4 am
No food
Only death to greet me
My family was behind the revolving door on
The other side of the precinct
Couldn't reach me
Only advocate
But death kept surrounding me in that
Cell
All rooted in trying to save someone
System set up to penalize through

Backwards rules giving authority of parenting to ACS Prisons
Oh, yea death tried to take me out that day in that cell
Until my brilliant, fine, and young Jewish Lawyer saved me from the crucifixion
So no thank you death not that jail cell
That day gave me back my power, girl power, Black woman fighting power, from the womb
So no thank you to the day death surrounded my car and threw me in a jail cell without my diabetes and Chemo pill to rot in their hell
But God brought by some angels
Who was named Gates for me to walk through
Death couldn't catch up with me that day, but its ass licking tried hard

Calling black Hispanic female ego tripping cop

Weaker n weaker
Pain in my breast
Refusing EMS
Help

THE WALL OF HOPE

Looking out of window of a view of a brick wall'
No light
Why was that
The suicides of the many students in college
Fretting over perfection
Being bullied over sexuality
Feeling shameful of who they love
Or not knowing how to love
Cause the Brick Wall stops
The sunlight
The brick wall stops
Breathing
One day she and a bunch of girls
Began throwing dots
Curses
Transformed into affirmations
Of climbing over the wall or under it
Or tearing it down in order
To stand without falling or wanting to jump
A March in the Village then to the Capital then to Washington to stop
Perfection and the pressures of Mental Sadness to Equip students no more
with just academic expectations but emotional solutions that details self-
medication of all-night cocaine Methamphetamine Hennessy, Vodka
shots, beer, and weed time to break the brick wall and make it a wall of
hope to touch feel be rise without drowning
No More Wall of Dope

More Doped up We Are
The More our Babies become
Dead black family extinct
Black woman powerless
The wall of Hope stands because
Of she

We stopped the pedophile
The molester of teenage girls
Abusing his power as an Assistant Attorney
Black Women Shut It Down
and it will Be Black Women who will rebuild the wall of hope
Knocking down inch by inch the Wall of Dope
It began on Wall Street Slave blocks to the White House to the Jail House
to

Certain Church Houses/ No More Wall of Dope
Good bye
A rebirth from the walls of the black woman has started the new wall of
hope for all to help rebuild

PENNIE ANNIE

1 West Dinner Theatre in Harlem where she performed as a Heroin addict through Dance sold out every night. She was only 17 years of age. Sold out every night to see the Heroine addict be portrayed so deeply and realistically through choreo poem formation that it brought tears to the audience's hearts.

Now the audience looks at the leader of this country as if addicted to
Pennsylvania Avenue freak show
Or belly of the beast
Or experiencing the illusion of a Shakespeare tragedy satire
or comedy through the big screen TV is Media Political Cable News

- Is it a farce, is it a lie, is it surreal?

Hell, it is tonight's First Union address of 2018?
But when I think of Union I think of freedom
I think of
Calvary, I think of Sojourner Truth "Ain't I a Woman?"
I think of Abolitionist
I think of HBCU's
Booker T. Washington
W.E.B. Dubois
Maya Angelou and Still I Rise with all this in power in my thighs to move a nation silently but Fiercely with Force like Makeda Queen of Sheba
A Harriet Tubman Freedom
And Frederick Douglass Union with President Lincoln

Not White Red Supremacist
The Black Wall Street of Tulsa Oklahoma
Flourished Rosewood town of Florida burnt down by a lie
A white woman lies of a black man 'cause she was drawn to the black genitals
Like baby boy Emmitt Till
"Take Back America Again Make it White Male Master Enslaved Again like what was done In Tulsa Rosewood Across 'tis America

I think of Reconstruction
I think of Black Panther
Black Sphinx
I think of Pyramids
I think of Diamonds in my backyard From South Africa to Sierra Leone

Malcolm King
I think of Harriet
I think of my children
I read about it
I had my grandfather tell me stories about them

those men in the south that pledged allegiance to the confederate flag

With economics free labor in exchange for lasers to your back stripped but naked
and pushing their confederate genitals between the throat of a black girl
and black mother's cheeks and thighs rough hard violently with liquor and
their pissy sweaty dirty bodies smothering a black girl or black mother
while a brother and father imprisoned to bow down
to be castrated to be hung from a tree with forced testicles jabbed into his mouth
fire cross burnt and live burnt skin crackling
roped whipped
Even the white men took turns sodomizing the black male
raped too
cause his clothes Skin stripped
blood red like hailstorm
 usually in a public mob with
black male testicles cut jabbed in mouth
with wife and Daughter standing there

So tonight, when I think of the Union address
I see the DACA Garcia family being sold, raped, and violated with you
know that family on TV two weeks ago in which parents brought him over
at 10 years old
illegally quote unquote now married to his citizen wife Son and Daughter teens
The ten-year-old who is now a man
 Owns his legitimate business
 but publicly lynched back to Mexico with his babies crying at the JFK airport
killing a Union
cause when I think of the simplest meaning of Union
It is a family
and Making America White again when they too were immigrants but did
confederate lynchings that have diseased itself as a contagious genocide
called Union address from the mouth of the one who said Make America Great Again
The One by Grabbing them by the pussy

81

so, Union address has a new dirty dreadful meaning for me tonight

It is more than just a white lie
Or a Farce
Or A Drug
It is a Shakespearean Tragedy Reality
We as players getting played
Into a Public Lynch Mob

KID CRACK PARENTING

No more kid crack
Helicopter mom
No more piloting
No more Engineering
No more promoting
Listening more
Less directing
More focusing on me myself and I
Letting go
Unavailable more
Yelling less
Dancing more
Holding me
Letting go of you
Living for me
Loving me
Shedding more
Embracing your fall only
If resuscitation is involved
Crying less
Laughing more
Facilitated by my logic & not my heart
Guarding my emotions.
But always praying harder than ever before

Cause I only carried you as my life.
God allowed you to be life I only nurtured
And fed my blood of sweat labor for an assigned time
God is doing the rest

I'm just the disciple goddess
Awaiting expecting prayerful results and gainful fulfilled blanks
Open arms if need be but closed door for now

Cause you baby boy baby girl will have your own doors and walks to push
through or climb over or blow to pieces in order to rebuild anew.

BITTER SWEET BABY GRADUATE

It was yesterday,
SHE
                                    held you in
HER
                        arms
Crying
  with laughter
                        and
fear
Knowing
                        SHE
bore the most
Fierce
WANTED
Being on planet universe
a Black
Male
Boy
                                        Child

SHE
laughed
and
cried
Knowing
                the labor
THE conscious
                                        strategic Chess moves
required mastery in her parenting.
 Hip
She belted an acapella
Moan Cry

Southern Blues
 Enslavement
 Grandma, Great Grandma
on her knees moan cry blues
 IF you are black Nubian indigenous woman mother
you feel me
YOU FEEL MY FEARS
My Explanation of Hopeless
but knowing all awhile
my strategic makeup

come up
of fostered advocated built up
                    of
My Black Son.
                              His skin tone of yellow
does not negate

the fear nor
Subside
Imprisonment
Future
at any minute in
Tis country Of America the Beautiful
called
does
"Black
Lives
Really
Matter?"

85

Streets

BLACK PRINCE: [IN DEDICATION TO RODNEY]

As I bent down
To identity his body
That summer night,
All I could remember
Was this smart boy
From my brother's class.
Rodney practically
Lived at our house
When I was growing up.
He was straight up honest and comical
He was always reminding me
How I should not
Look down
On that girl
Who was
In the hospital
With me.
"She always talks about you. How you encouraged her
And inspired her to believe in herself."
There are certain things you want to forget about that had taken place in
your life.
I began to play
Back in my head when Rodney was driving BMW's
And Jeeps
Straight off the lot
In the late 80's
When I use to visit home
From college.   I will never forget

When he began experiencing with the crack
he was selling.

 "Crack" had taken him to Another Level.
I bumped into him on the elevator in Lincoln Projects
He smelled and looked like
He had not bathed for days
I just froze
Just like I am now
Standing
Looking into his face.
This time
He is lying

On the floor dead,
Instead of
The walking dead, walking dead.
I just froze.
As I bent looking at Him on the floor dead
Cold Blood
His Own Blood. With his shirt, off
The police stood in the room
As if they were babysitting
Monitoring a class of black
Dying Men before their 30's
Swimming
 Dying
 Drowning
in
Their own
 Dead   blood!

Fly Soar with Your Black Wings
Now You are Free to Fly, Soar,
And Reach a Plain that Could Not Fully be Achieved here.
Black Prince imprisoned in a time
A Frame of mind of circumstances
Beyond control. No More Shackles.
Your talents and gifts that were embedded in your soul
From the beginning.
Embodied into your mother's womb rapture!!!
Can no longer be stripped
Trapped
Tricked
Deceived.

The Demons can no longer plague, revisit,
Your Journey is on the other side.
Your Essence
      Presence
              Honesty
Consciousness of your Situation
Can no Longer tear away the pain,
      The realities of chains
    Not being able to
              Release
                   Retrieve
                   Revive

Black Prince
You are Our Reality
OF WHAT ROAD WE CHOOSE
WOULD like to Choose
But Another has been Chosen
When that moment came knocking at your spirit
All that was yesterday was removed
Chains broken
Shackles relinquished
Soul purified
Body Cleansed
And the Black Prince You are
Shined, Soared Sparked
Into a Higher, Reuniting Spirit of Oneness with the Creator
Flying, Soaring with your Black Wings.

Your 6ft 5 Demeanor
                    Laughter
        Smile
Dimples
        Jokes
Sensitivity
        Support
Realness
    High IQ Brilliance
Will never Perish, but Cherished to the heart
 Every time I teach a black boy in a blackboard classroom.

MS. PIPER
Piped
Smoked and
Coked
Sniffed and
Licked
Mr. Pecker's
Dick
Ms. Piper
Young
And   Strung
Cause 5 minutes highs
Freed Demons
Rampant in her mind
Whatever it takes
For Ms. Piper lips
To Smoke the Pipe
First must sleep with
Peter Pecker's wife
Lick it right
Walking bare
In the daylight air
Young girls see
Ms. Piper's Flair
Torn and Beaten
Turned Outside in
Now living
The street life
Of Piped Dreams
Beauty bound   Psyched choked
Soul imprisoned
Ms. Piper discovered
The reality
Of no more
Nursery Rhymes
When you sniff

Peck
Lick
And   smoke
The Pipe
Forever
Enslaved to Mr. Pecker   and His Wife!

90

IT PAINS ME BROTHER SISTER (1990)

It pains me to see you standing there naked, (Defenseless)
Your master is no longer yourself.
Your master s no longer love.
Your master is no longer your children.
Your master is no longer your job.
Your master is no longer your family.

YOUR MASTER IS NOW AND ALWAYS TILL DEATH DO US PART: "CRACK"

You just stand there. (Defenseless.)
You give up your manhood.
She gives up her womanhood.

The babies become contaminated.
The babies become corrupted.
The babies become dead.

Why Brother Man, Why Sister Soul?
Your master is now and forever do us part that hard, whited sadistic demonic crack.

I hear that "the crack" sells your womb.
I hear that your children are auctioned off into foster homes.

It pains me brother! You can no longer produce.
You can no longer procreate
It pains me you can no longer articulate.
Your words,
Your soul,
Your spirit,
Your mind,
All has been hijacked kidnapped to that hard-white pale demonic sadistic Master, Crack!
It pains me my sister!
You have become the breeders of your Master.
No longer is it the or time in a history book.
Or is it them and time in a history book?
It is hard stiff white sadistic patriarchal white Master cum Crack!
He whips you
He pimps you with strangers
He contaminates the womb

91

You no longer know what father from what child
Master Enslavement Plan

But it doesn't matter anymore.
They are still raping and having us any which way they can
When it is done to you
It is done to me sister

That hard bitch sadistic master chokes the rape into you
It makes you pimp off your sacred womb with breast no longer able to
shoot out nutrients

Every brown baby born is taken from you
It is sold. It is auctioned off to the best buyer
 a designed failed school system
A corporate prison system
a molested foster care
A perpetuated drug Generation X.

That hard-sadistic white patriarchal genital has historically done it again.
You have allowed it to blindly with assimilation and brokenness to violate
(invade)
Through penetration of a pipe into your mind and body.
    Oh, how It pains me my sister!

You have given birth
You have given still birth
You have given Abortion
You have born crack out of your womb
You have corrupted the fetus
You have killed your spirit
You have died inside out
Why brother, sister WHY?
    You don't know!
  And Neither Do I!

BANKRUPTCY

When that train wreck comes
    Bankruptcy follows
No resources to run to anymore
Black Women have to fight

As their
Bodies filled with hands tied up
Minds diseased
Why fixated by white wash juxtaposed by brain washed
   compelled to save And
Stand by their so-called man
While pimped out
                    sold out
on an auction block
Created by
patriarchal SCUM CUM
why?
As a ride or die chick?
Loyalty
Looking at the Feds
Danbury
Brooklyn
Manhattan jails

Beautiful stunning women of blackness women of brown Caramel
chocolate almond straight curly kinky long short hair
 Natural
 Curvy
 Lean
Round
                    Tall
                       Short
Articulate
Their eyes revealed the soul of empty
Loss dismayed pain
Laughter, tears,
blood pours down into the sitting waiting room
Manage
Self-care
Awareness
A tyrant Trust
Tribe team

93

I wailed in the car then in their bathroom then through my drive back home
with consolation following a migraine
Didn't let them see
I wailed how can I help me
Sisters
Dressed in their khakis

                              name replaced by a number

identity choked by a man
who rearranged their smiles
Into a different type of death.

GAMBLING WOMAN

Needles weren't her thing
Coke was too fast
Crack made no sense
Grass slowed her down
The red white green dice
The blue red white ice
Spotted dice
Checkered Cards
Queen of Spades
   Queen of Diamonds
Queen of Hearts
   Queen of Clubs
Jokers Wild
That was her thing!

 Legs Long, Curvy and skinny
 Heavy on top
Tall Big and Confidant
Brown Skin
Light Brown Eyes
Carrying it well
Gambling Woman

By 21 accepted into New York Law School
Received her Broker's Licensed in Real Estate in the 70's
Graduating from Ivy League College
With some of the Kennedy Girls
Never going into Law School
Becoming a Real Estate Broker by 25.
Giving birth to 3 black boys by a Dominican she
Had no desire to marry
Owning her own house at the age of 23
Gambling Woman

Raising her boys
With a No-Nonsense Fist
Loving them Hard
And
Cutting them with her hand
On Demand
Later marrying a Basin man
Giving birth to her daughter

Gambling Woman had weekend card parties from Friday
Night straight to Sunday morning
Against her husband wishes

Doing this   before   he came along
Making money   to   pay mortgage
   Support family
Having plenty to   Spare
Big brown girl
Called gambling woman

Would go head to head with any man
Not blinking
Or Unfolding
Even with a man pointing a gun to her head
        In a Gambling Hall
Gambling Woman

   Gambling   Woman

G a m b l I n g   Woman

DEMANDING
Thief
Gun in hand
Fearless Woman
Gambling Woman
Not letting go
Gambling bullets to her head
Now Leaving 4 children
With no more

G A M B L I N G   M A M A!

#Confirmations

CAPTIVITY

When you share your dreams
Or your talents
Don't let it be in a careless space
Or share it with Insecure Hands.
Those hands can hold you in captivity;
It can attempt to strangle
You lifeless;
Layer yourself with armor
The Kind
That is
Only
Visible to YOU.

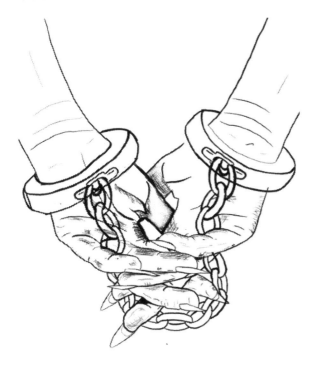

THE GOOD FIGHT

Fight reflectively
Fight seeking
Fight Sharing
Fight Caring
Fight loving
Fight by medicating the wounds
Through a massive peeling.
Fight speaking
Fight living
Fight Truth
Fight Silence
You know when you done depleted
cause lies run like atoms all around you
*Some rampant in your mind from snakes draped as Humanity furnished with jealously
insecurity*
Fight Space
Fight Liars
Fight Jealousy
Fight insecurity
Fight ugly
Fight beauty
Fight rapist
Fight contamination
Fight disease
Fight hate
Fight Nasty
Fight gossip
Forget seasons
Be present
NOW1

STAYING POWER

When you hear those inspiration words
And feel as though nothing can stop you.
You find yourself in a sacred space hanging on to every scripture
affirmation which validates your existence to a greater destination
regardless of circumstances.
Pushing leaning and running forward.
Reminding yourself it isn't a marathon or a race.
Time will not wait,
But it will stand for you to sit down.
Believing that self-actualization
It is just you plant yourself to visualize
That you are
And will do
And feel
And see
And be.
Make it positive with truth.
Truth is subjective sometime
in order to become objective about your created reality.
Memories become slurred or categorized into pictures.
Cartoon caricatures.
Don't compare yourself to anyone.
Their journey is not yours and your destination is a temporary means to a
better end.

Another way of putting it
When you hear scattered words
Integrated with clamoring cruelty
Don't be dismayed.
Sign off and build your Breakthrough

ISOLATION

Walks taken by yourself
Are not considered the loneliest
Remove self-dying in the movement
Motionless but still walking toward it
Some walks are prerequisites to your requiem
Automatic systematically gravitated by your inner chemist
 to attract your outer seamstress.
Sews you up to fit into a fashionista box
not always decorated with attraction.
BUT distracting atoms

                            have you float further out to sea?

Floating journey walks
May rewrite a swim

Close drown the air

Earth

&

SHAKE YOU INTO A WHIRLWIND

WAR FARE

Fearful is a disease
It kills creativity
 Deadens mobility
Cripples clarity
Attracts dream killers
Makes up lies
So, you make yourself believe it is true;
Will make you hide under sheer mask
 Falsify your dreams into nightmares
Bankrupted and Hijacked
You band together
And Delete it with Force
Fear will break you to
BROKENNESS
Every fiber in your
Body
Mind
And Spirit must replace it
 with Faith
 BUT- faith takes more work
It isn't a **Fantasy**
Of
Sort

I CAN DO ALL THINGS
THROUGH JESUS CHRIST
WHO STRENGTHENS ME

While man tried to Deplete Me
And the Devil tried to strangle me with the Big "C"
As Cancer Entered my Body
not once,
but twice,
but three strikes you're out!

My J.C. had his handle on me

I Can Do All Things Through Jesus Christ Who Strengthens Me

While man tried to Depress Me
And the devil attempted to Oppressed me
With the disease
 Of the

Big "C"

While Chemo stripped me of good cells
            Jesus replenished me with new cells
Unleashing all the deadness
&
Decay that tried to manipulate
My Body,
Spirit
& Soul
Jesus Retaliated
in favor
of me
His Armor
became
the Surgeon
 Oncologist
   Counselor
He Nursed

                                                  the fears

the endless tears,

the countless nights
the pain endeared!

**I can do All Things through Jesus Christ
who strengthens Me**

Through all of my Solace Nights

Who Empowers me to be
The Strong Black Mother in
Which He Assigned
for Me

My Goddess Isis
And my First-Born Prince
Imani on each of my hip

It was only Jesus Christ who strengthens me to be
To see
To discern
To believe
Endure
Embrace
And Give Praise
In the
DARKEST
BLACKEST
MEEKEST
MUDDY STORM
of the
the battlefield where the 3 "deadly "D" s:
DISEASE,
DIVORCE,
DEPRESSION
Tried To Kill Me
Topping it off
with the
Big C.
God said,
"NO!"
&   Resurrected Me!
But like the Modern Woman of Ancient Times,
Of my Southern Harlem Roots,
& African Blood
Running
through

my Veins,
Only J.C> was there

To catch me from the pits of hell

Strengthened
&
Restored ME

To Continue on to Complete
MY

ASSIGNED DESTINY!!!!!

EMPTY LIPSTICK

Stop holding on to stuff that got nothing in it!

Why keep it in your purse
or digging at the bottom to touch your lips?
 Realize and trust
It no longer serves your lips
 or enhance your beauty
which resides in
Giving birth outwards
every time.
You digging your fingers all in it -
to get something out of it
 'cause you think you saving yourself from a debt
By not traveling shopping & purchasing something new
In essence
what are you really doing?

Actually, preventing yourself from being the glamour fabulous mountain
climber champion beauty you!
Reinvestment in You
it's a necessity!
If not
                                will result
into a liability
a pricey commodity.
 Time baby girl, to renew the color in you
Stop holding on to the empty barrel of
"IT"
or
" HIM"
or
"THAT"
or
"SHE"
or
"TOXIC THOUGHTS"
that got nothing
to do
with you
anymore!
"That was about your THEN"
"This about your NOW!"

Try rekindling your ZEN

Your life it is the most important investment ever to be made in History
No, not their story
or *his* story
or *her* story
or narrative
or pieces of fragments of
their watered-down truth of your journey!

Time to invest in the Best…. You baby girl!

Stop holding on to stuff that got nothing in it!!!

 Why replace something of no value that has already been used, reused,
done and hold on to it?

Regardless of
IT
or HE
or SHE
or THEM
or THOUGHT
or SEASON
or JOB
or LOVER
THEY HAVE SERVED ITS PURPOSE

For the
Yesterday
That is
good
and gone!

Every glow
                              tear
                                        touch
pain
laughter
dance
 song
 Requiem death
intensely creating a jazz blues flow
to your skin heartfelt soul

Best believe was for
a required reason
Required season
And required Lesson to be written in your history book....

Your lips are too beautiful
It can no longer afford to hold to empty
Or sucked pipes

Act with
discernment
 Dance rhythmically with haste:
to release
Dismantle
this empty weight,
First,
Do not save it for the earth to recycle.
Second,
Throw it in the garbage
Stop reminiscing how it was exclusively for your lips and skin
to pop,
remember
 that was then
THIS IS NOW!
Third,
You are only to be filled up with diamonds, gold, crystal, African ancient
anointments and good wine
 Never to perish,
but gets better with time.
 Let go of that stuff at the bottom of your expensive pocketbook
called
empty   weight.
It will drown you.

Let it go!
I'm watching!
 The children are watching.
                                        Before throwing it in the garbage

burn it.
Whatever you do
or
however, you do,

Just Do!
Just release it
from you!

Never to look back, embrace, taste again to your beautiful red lips!

#BlackTOO

UNSPOKEN

Whisper through your moves

Night owl storms she refused let him hear her tears. Daddy worked too hard made too many sacrifices. Between driving the NYC Trains Cabs on the weekend catering parties and running numbers there was no way she could let him see those tears. She whispered in her sleep she wept in the tub while the water ran. She knew if daddy would find out it would be some killing done. It was hard to articulate words the shame guilt the anxiety felt.

How do you explain an unwanted touch when you do not really have a voice yet? How can you explain the blood that leaves no stains but heartfelt heartache? Daddy could never know cause the family would be torn apart. The older male Cousin the teenage boy at the park her friend's male cousin who was babysitting she and her friend New Year's Eve then one day pulled in the boiler room where the neighbor down the block thought it okay to put his penis rubbed against her backside about to penetrate but someone came, and she was able to run. She ran till next year into last week. She buried it away. She mustn't forget the Cousin who went on a bad acid trip and felt her up and made her sit on top of him naked in the middle of the living room; her only 9 and him 20 something.

She found a new escape. Her dance her art. She dances on empty beer cans rejecting the pollution that almost took her out. Now when they start this #MeToo Movement wearing all black she wonders at almost half a century why now and not then?

111

PTSD

With the good old boys' club
We as woman can be young beautiful smart
 open ourselves to a man\
 put in grind coach lead
 and not any man
 it is usually your man your soulmate husband
And he can one day just leave with all your insides with him
 start a new life new children new family and MIA!
For argument sake
Leaving your babies
Disrespecting the mother of your children
Just Never Ends Well
It goes deep
Therapist say well if he has abandonment issues and his parents were
unavailable physically and emotionally in early childhood trauma scars are
perpetuated
One would think if my daddy wasn't there I'm a be there for my children
Please do not tell me about the fact he is educated and a therapist now, so
he should know better it is so redundant in the hood; my Godmother calls
it NiggerEducated
But if you never recognized your pain or dark molested abusive nights
without real help because
society doesn't create a space for   Black brown boys to cry the whispers
and secrets of raped stuck or touched by the same gender in the anal or oral
by another or when revealed almost beat to death cause no one was there to
save them or the deep dark terror experience by a boy who is now a man,
but the boy is untreated inside the man
When does the cycle stop?

It began with She the single divorced black mother aware to have her son
and Daughter always equipped with the Resources of therapy truth and
God
To break the cycle.
Treatment before crisis
Prepares crisis
To be dealt
 with effectively Not scarcely!

BASEMENT

He was so dam cute!
Her cheeks turned red in his presence
Cause he was the finest 6"5 ft
Tall curly hair
Light hazel eyes cocoa brown skin
Basketball star
F I N E
All the girls wanted his look touch
and
to be
the one
One day
A hot day
In Brooklyn Bed Sty
As she sat on the fire escape
in her landmark tenement
Building
Kids from around the way played
Outside on the fire hydrant shooting water
Some played stick ball
Others
Double Dutch to the hip hop beats of Sugar Hill
as Brother Raheem
sold beam pies
Telling every black girl who strolled by in Bedsty
"You are Queens
your bodies like temples
to be
worshipped
your minds like diamonds
not
to be
exploited."
We black girls giggled: Shanequa Tany and I
They laughed at Raheem
But girl when Curly hair 6'5 Dickie came dribbling that ball winking his eye
at us with them big beautiful black hands
long fingers manicured nails
Big feet with the latest high-top sneaks
We just melted
Panties wet melted
Dressing to impress

With my tight bell bottom jeans tank top Afro puffs candy lip gloss
popping gum
Finally
He said,
"Come here Beautiful... let's go for a walk"
We ended in that basement
Me Excited
Dickie said, "Take your clothes off."
Hesitantly I did.
Leaving panties and bra on
"No all of it!" He said.
Yes, my first time with my Crush basketball Prince Star
A Black Out
He quickly rolled my clothes up like a basketball while running and laughing
up the stairs.
Left naked in the basement
bare
crying
knowing mama gonna
Tear my fast ass up
for
even going
in the
basement
with
a boy
Looked in hallway on my fifth floor
Tearfully
Running to my apartment door
4 E Naked and all
Took keys out
shaking like a Junkie
Thanking God
for the
black out
No lights
Just darkness
My darkness
to match
black out darkness
in bare hallway
With my bare soul
naked body
Mama worked nights

Ran to bathroom
Took a hot
burning
scourging
shower
to scrub the dirt
while punishing me
of his #MeToo
Fucking Sick
insane nastiness
Never to tell a soul
not even My best friends
Shanequa and Tanya
and definitely not
my ass
whipping
Black Mama!

AUDITION

Realizing Baring it All
How Could she
When the bareness became barren
Stripped unveiled getting goose bumps
Running into the bathroom panicking panic attacks
Not realizing the reality of unveiling her most vulnerable G- Spot on stage.
Some say Vagina Monologues is her expertise
She mustn't allow the Voyeurism of them

Eyes to Objectify her thighs
        Nor behind
 Cause her Breast Reconstructed
One bigger than the other
Metastasized

THE AUDITION
Is Masking Unmasking layers of skin caused by a lack of estrogen?
Multiplied Suffocated by test-- -os- -- te-rone

Hey Ebony, Brown, Yellow Red Gal......
This Audition is Revolutionized into Silence
No one told you we have a camera with Lens
That take NO Pictures
But Shoot dots at your Ebony Brown Yellow Red Skin.
Don't worry about your pay
For this work
Cause Once You make the CUT
In this   HOLlywood   PRODUCtion
We are filming only Chocolate Bunnies
With no script
Directed to Open Your Legs REAL WIDE
Not for a STRETCH or GRAND PLIE
But to be Ostracized
It is Not Rape When Paid
Or
Doped to PLAY?
Audition yes, it is Legit!
Cause Rules made up by White Men
Smoking cigars to NOT Give Grammy's Oscars to your Objectified
Voyeuristic Hip, Tit, Ass, Leg. They can't see your mind or hear your voice
But how far you can open your mouth
To take in their unwanted patriarchal
Dominant
Genital CUM
Hush Don't tell a Soul Cause you must remember

You are property
At the bottom
Of their
Totem Pole
Historically
Taught CAN DO
HAVE YOU
Any which way
FRONT, BENT, or BACK
No Worries

Only an Illusion
Called "Audition"

117

SILENT CORNER

The music was loud. The song in her bosom echoed so strong and hard. The pain was unbearable. All she knew is that this beautiful thing, created growing inside of her needed to be born out of love. It was created out of a plan; a bond of matrimonial bliss, slaughtered in a heartbeat of a second. Star knew this unborn child needed to be born with no marks of insecurity; to stifle her beauty in spite of her father's adulterous, abusive, and opportunist lifestyle. Solomon became a ghost dancing on beer cans trying to fit. Desperately trying to eat caviar to fit in, while throwing up on cheap champagne. He put some strong seeds in Star's womb. He tried to create an asylum for her. His superego tried to create a wall, a cage to imprison her mind, spirit, soul, and crown.

Why did he try to create a public portrait to his colleagues, friends and his Haitian clean-up woman who he was having an affair during this evolution? He created the script as though Star was the unstable one; the hysterical pregnant wife. He had to clean up his image and justify why he tried to kill his pregnant wife. Why he tried to **"to kill this black bitch?"** The babies they planned and the marriage that he begged to take place. The irony is he could not leave New York City to his next Navy assignment, without having Star as his. Now Star understood what her Grandpa Elijah used to say and have endless sermons with her parents on family background. He believed background is everything. **"If a child comes from weak roots, broken branches, and street corners with junkie dreams; that child will grow to exemplify those same dreams."** Grandpa Elijah stood on this affirmation as a non-negotiable. He and the old folks sat on the porch of southern ancestry believed if you lay down with needles, it enters into your blood, and can kill you.

Star did not want to believe this. She did not come from that school of thought. She felt one is judged by their actions, ambitions, love songs, and not by the demons that haunt them cause of their family misplaced accomplishments or bad choices.

Star sat down on the floor of her bedroom and began pouring the words into her journal:

There is so much buried inside of me. Deep. Deep inside… Yes Pain! Incomplete. Back and forth, in and out.!"
Allowing Solomon to come into her life was part of the cycle. The worst was in Washington D.C., five months pregnant with Egypt. Egypt is a blessing. Yes Lawd. A beauty of a blessing.
Everything came full circle; the fight in front of their three- and half-year-old son with him choking her, blood gushing out of her mouth. Star

running out of their military base townhouse for her life through the snow dripping blood on the base. Her blood on the white snow; his bare hands went too far stayed too long. The abandonment of Solomon just leaving her to die on the military base with no food, money, or love to be nourished. She knew that her God had another plan. She needed to see what this man was really capable of. How far would he really go? She fell into a deep depression of rage, sadness, and shock; but all the while she kept moving, searching, and fighting until the moon made her go to the sun, back to her home in Hampton Virginia.

The psychiatrist on the base wanted to cover up what Solomon did to her by labeling scars onto Star as post-traumatic stress, depression, but never facing the why? Why is it Solomon masked layers of his demons stripped her saneness?

Yes, she could have gone back to New York. She could have gone back to Harlem; to Striver's Row to live with her parents; however, she chose to stay with her husband.

Star needed to discover what she was dealing with after the fight. She sent Osiris to her parents. She still thought Solomon and her could sew their marriage back together. All she knew she was very pregnant by him; a planned pregnancy.

She recalls the summer so well. He told their family and friends how he wanted them to have a little girl. How he and Star was going to make another baby. How Star made such pretty babies. She should have analyzed the prior statement. How in the hell can Star make pretty babies, when it takes both of them.? He left her in the ghetto of D.C. to die! It felt like a burning knife cutting Star to the womb of her core. She swallowed the hurt and threw up fighting.

She just wanted him to come home and say, **"Baby we will get through this together. I love you, because I married you. You still are my Queen, my B.A.P My Black African American Princess."**

Reality is one hell of a thing. She had their child in her womb and he wanted her in shackles. He tried to have her put into an asylum on the Air Force Base and deliver Egypt in a fucking asylum. She didn't know if it was because he was almost delivered in a gypsy cab as a heroin baby and wanted the same generation curse in his children's life. It was too painful and deep.

She can still remember the psychiatrist at the Naval Hospital saying, **"You need some rest. This is the best place for you. You are safe from your husband here. We are here to protect you."**

This was a nightmare. Star is a civilian and her husband secretly signed her in. In the middle of the night she had taken a cab to the hospital from the base. She called Solomon at his brother's house to take her to the hospital. He told her he was not coming and to have the ambulance pick her up. She thought her water broke. She was having severe pains, while her panties were soaking wet. She was spotting. Star ended up in the military hospital in the emergency room. She was in the O.B.G.Y.N section. The next thing she knew she saw this tall skinny white male doctor on the phone talking to her husband about her prognosis. They kept her hooked up to some machine that monitored the baby. Her blood pressure had shot up. Star was kept overnight in the O.B.G.Y.N unit. Early the next morning she saw that same doctor she had seen talking to Solomon on the telephone last night. The doctor began shifting his energy to a condescending tone. This white male patriarchal doctor began telling Star she was in the best care now. She did not have to worry anymore.

Star thought, **"What the hell was he talking about? "**
She looked on his photo I.D and saw that he was a damn Psychiatrist. Star began crying and screaming. Her husband tried to beat her ass on the military base. Now, she is in the Military Hospital about to be put to silenced!

~

Innocence was she..
It was the unborn fetus
Growing inside her womb.
Star was glowing,
When she found out
she was in the family way.
Solomon is going to be so happy
She thought.
He was coming in a timely fashion.
Once he received the news.
He was becoming more estranged.
Solomon almost drove her
to destroy two spirits.
The unborn innocence, and herself.

"I'm lost. It is so painful. You get lost in telling."

Thought Star as she recalls her
Mama holding her as she fell into a pit.

Mama was on her knees in her bedroom crying.

She was hesitant when Star came in.
 Star thought she had seen death staring her in the face.

120

Cause mama was in a fetus-
kneeling trance
prayerful way.

From her southern upbringing,
this was part of her prayerful ritual.
That is
Crying,
Screaming,
and Speaking aloud in Tongues...

Usually after this,
she would be in a joyful way.

Not this time.

Mama was rewinding the scene back in her mind.

 When he found out the baby was coming, Solomon had become demonic.

This boy had cursed out his God.
Thought Star's Mama.

"He said to me", the Mother of Star,

"This is the last thing I need to hear!"
Innocence she was.
It was the unborn fetus
growing inside her womb.

Then this boy tries to reverse the guilt on me,

Her Mama!

Solomon said:

"Why did you tell her what I said?"

"First and foremost why did you say that? Take responsibility for your words."
Mama said with hips on hand,
back arched
head regally wrapped.

"Is she pregnant, that is the last thing I need to hear."

"Those aren't her Mama words. Those are your words. I had to bring her back to reality!"

Star thought it was Love making, when it was more like fuck making.

"Wounded but not Defeated she sang this song."

The inner voice of Star rang loud and strong in her subconscious knocking against the window pane of her conscious. Rejection has had somewhat of an impact in Star's life, that she had almost come to the point of tossing her dreams to the wind. During her career as a commercial model, actress, and dancer in New York City, she had been wounded many times with bullets such as: "You look too young," "You look too old," and "We are not looking for any BLACK girls at this time." On the other side, agents who seemed interested in her, turned out out to be more interested in getting her into their bedroom, or perpetrating a facade. They were con artist whose expertise is to take advantage of naive, eager, young innocent and aspiring artist to blow up their own pockets as they suction the victims flat. Their lines are: "We can't use these pictures: We design our own portfolio for you; four hundred, five hundred dollars," and this is the end of their bargain.

At sixteen years of age, Star had to create and define her own space, boundaries, limitations, and expectations. They were very high!

Yet faith, hope, and motivation had a funny way of propelling Star to quickly get up from her falls, cure her own bruises, and continue in the pursuit and realization of her dreams.

Now at 29 years old she knew, like great Grandma Maggie had taught her Grandma Caroline, and her Mama Queen, had taught her. That is: "To hold fast and clench her dreams into her fist and bury it deep down into her bosom." She could no longer live inside herself.
Star had no choice but to be open to the world and those around her. Her emotions ran so deep, especially these past 10 years of her life, that the only way she could fully express them to her fullest, is through her innate God-given talents. She knew now, more than ever, she would not allow herself to be defeated. No-one, not even Solomon could take her into a contaminated battered space of mind or asylum spirit.
Pain will make you humble to your knees. Star realized that only life could

teach her the harsh realities of survival. Family was everything. She didn't realize that her husband did not come from the same umbilical cord that she was born from. She did not know what she knows now.

Pain took her to the next level. Tears of blood dripped from her mouth that night while her precious seed implanted by what she thought was her love making; *Soulmating* penetrating her womb. She was six months pregnant with their second child, While he ran his arms around her neck. All she could see then was a nigger. A beast sweating with madness, trying to give her an instant abortion with his eyes, fist, his words:

"I'm gonna kill this bitch. This BLACK bitch who I begged to marry me I thought I could control. This black bitch, the mother of my Faith: I'm gonna kill the very essence of her spirit. Crazy, stank bitch. Think you too good, Too smart. When I met you, you were Ms. Educator, Intellectual, Sensitive twenty-two years old who graduated at the top of her class at 21 years of age with a B.A. in English, a concentration in Print Media/ Journalism and a Minor in Speech and theatre."

This kept running in and out of Star conscious half hearing him, while coming up for air to breathe; To fight to live.

*   *   *   *

Star stood on the telephone in her kente, cloth wrapped around her body, asking him when the hell he was coming back home. They needed to talk and go to therapy. She had taken a leave of absence from her job to fly to D.C. to make her marriage work. Star was a young black girl who had the world on her shoulders. She was exposed to it all. Before him, she had a top college prep well- rounded kind of southern Harlem black girl strong family love tribe village growing up. She was what one consider B.A.M.P that is what he use to call her when the romance what hot, heated, filled with good tasting spicy fury kind of love. They would go dancing in clubs, go to the Broadway theatre frequently in New York City. She excited him. She was a mystery. During their courting she was real reserved, observant, eloquent, articulate, and a kind of bodacious, boldness ,meekness, kinds of essence!

"Solomon, what do you mean I am a B.A.M.P.! This is a new acronym for me. Please be more direct. I am trying to follow you and connect with the words and your voice. Was this another self-help book you read. Wait I know what you mean You mean a Buppie."

"No Star I mean A B.A.M.P.! Guess again."

"I give up," Said Star as they laughed over a lobster dinner.

She was laughing until she was crying. Those two strawberry daiquiris and one piña colada must have loosened some chromosomes up, because, dam, if she knew what a B.A.M.P. was. He was looking so innocent and cute. He reminded Star of a little boy who was trying to impress his teacher with his big vocabulary on the first day of school.

"You know Solomon I was never good with playing Jeopardy. Please tell me what it is. I hope it is good, however anxiety is making me want to dance it out of you."

"I am surprised an English teacher like you doesn't know the meaning of this acronym. Okay I will not let you suffer anymore. You are definitely a Black African-American Princess."

This was a new one for Star. Now people have said she is spoiled, high-spirited, graceful, high maintenance, Diva, Congenial, Ms. Queen, and host of other name callings or compliments; but never did she hear it defined into a acronym like this.

*   *   *   *

She secretly thought,

" Maybe he is a little intelligent. But he doesn't have to use fancy words that he read in all the self-help, codependency books to speak plain English. To tell you the God honest truth that day I didn't know whether to open myself up up to him, Or walk out of the restaurant. I just laughed and kinda changed the subject, cause Mama always said that if I didn't have anything nice to say, always be polite."

Star was thinking this in her head and not aloud. All the time she was smiling and being very attentive to his needs and autobiography. I just was not in the mood for the bullshit at this point in the game. I was twenty-two years old and tired of shaping the mind of these black men boys that came into my life. It would be nice to meet someone who did not feel threatened by you or if they liked you they became overtly too domineering to the essence of your spirit. I was in a relationship for five years to a fine young breed of a man boy; I had known since I was a big eyed chocolate baby in Harlem. He came from a refined family. He kept a good job. He maintained a nice Co-Op in Harlem on Riverside Drive overlooking the Hudson River.

I had the keys. He bought me all types of diamonds, a computer for my graduation out of High School; however in the late 1980's he was too committed to a white hard, evil, sadistic lady.

Her name was "**lady fucking devil crack.!**" I didn't know what the hell that was.

Yes I knew what cocaine was. I had friends and peers who sniffed it socially. I went to a very elite private high school on the Upper East Side in Manhattan. The irony of it all I intentionally chose to attend this all girls Catholic School off Park avenue, instead of going to La Guardia High School of the Performing Arts. I made this conscious choice, because I wanted to be more focused on my academics and stay away from the boys during the day. I still received intensive professional training in modern, ballet, jazz, and acting. I performed in several off Broadway Production Theaters during my time in High School. I had done some print work for Teen Magazine and went on many go sees, auditions and experienced freelance modeling work. I also was chosen to be the principal dancer to promote advertisement for one of the top performing arts schools in the city.

I was 16 years old about to enter 12th grade, when I bumped into Malcolm. He was a good bad boy then. A mixture of a Buppie, but underlying Harlem thug swag. He chased after me for months showering me with gifts and amazing dates. Horseback carriage ride in central park, dinner at Tavern on The Green, and gauging David Cookies down our throat after smoking weed with hysterical laughter. Yes jokes, and dancing all night at the Garage was one of the many highlights I experienced with him. He supported me in whatever I wanted to do, but all that time he had another woman on the side. Her name was first Cocaine; then it graduated to Ms. Crack. He literally hid it so well. By the time I knew that he was not a social occasional addict, I was 21 years old in my Senior of college year trying to get him the hell out of my life. I felt he had not grown any. I had totally forgotten everything my Mama taught me, that her Grandma Maggie taught her; And that is, never tell a black man straight out that you are leaving him. That Negro and yes I use the term very loosely, cause he did not digest the words very well. He went ballistic.! He became Spiderman, Batman and the Jokester all at the same time in a bad way. He started jumping out of bushes on my college campus, climbing trees stalking me. Showing up at a major radio news outlet where I was doing my college internship credits. Seeing his ass conveniently show up on the Staten Island Ferry at 6 am in the morning on my way to my intern from my college dorm, when he lived in Harlem.

Literally and figuratively ballistic. I can't remember if this was before I

125

found out I was pregnant two months before graduating college that I told him it was not going to happen. **The present was done and the future of us was never to be.** The night before the procedure, he stayed up all night in my dorm sitting at my desk looking at me while I slept. Every now and then I would wake up and this Negro was sitting with his legs crossed arm on his knee and hand on his face; sometimes crying. The more he cried, the more shelled in and numb I became. I could not feel or change this.

It had to be terminated and the next morning a Jewish white male doctor took care of it. Thank God I was under my father's insurance. I was able to get the best care on Park Avenue. Sitting in the waiting room with women who did not look like me and was in a higher financial bracket did not matter that day; we all had one thing in common. We had the choice to decide what to do with our fucking vagina, life, bodies, and even our minds.

"How could I bring a crack baby into this world? How could I have a baby and I am about to graduate college and soar towards my dreams? How can I do this with a black boy man child still in his gutter enslaved brokenness shackled demons?"

It was not fair for me, him, or that fetus. This was my first High School College sweetheart. Everyone including his family, my family, our fiends, and my subconscious thought marriage would be us. My spirit knew the dance and rhythm was off balanced. The ancestral voice spoke to me in dreams and in my reality of blood empty stain pain!

I could not tell a soul about this, except my brother. I only told him the water down version that I was pregnant.

His naive response, **"I am going to be an Uncle."**
I was like, **"No you are going to look out for the mail for me cause daddy health insurance is paying for this abortion and I do not want him to see it."**
He became deaden on the phone and we never discussed it again; as if it never happened. My brother and Malcolm became friends almost like brothers through our years of dating. Although my brother always knew that his allegiance was with his baby sister; we were ride or die all day, every day.

Mental abuse is a funny thing, because I can not put your hand on it. I can not see mental scars left, but they are like a mother. They are still with me, when everyone else is gone. Malcolm knew he could not put his hands on me because my brother and male cousins would beat his ass into a mother fucking pulp. Malcolm use the mind to break, control, and deceive me into deep layers of darkness. It was deep. He began taking refuge and fighting back with Voodoo. He was into that dam Santeria shit. I was very aware of my African Culture and the history of our religion before enslavement in mother Africa. I fell in love with Anthropology, Sociology, Black Literature, classes in High School and College. I did exceptionally will in African Studies, African-American Studies, Anthropology Amazon people in South America, the pygmies, African tribes throughout the diaspora, in which I did major research under renowned scholars and stellar Professors of African and African American History. My Professors in those classes urged me to change my major to Social Sciences.

No matter how educated you are in a subject, nothing in the world could prepare me for Malcolm and his Santeria rituals combined with being high off of cocaine, crack, and weed. This was my senior year in college. He started wearing all white, and turbans on his head reminding me of the Disney movie Aladdin, smoking cigars through the house, burning funny smelly incense, putting food by the door, and watering up several glasses' with beautiful flowers to put on what he called an altar in our living room. Even though I lived on campus, I would live during the summer, vacations, and sometime on the weekends at his apartment. It all depended on how I felt. The more I distanced myself, the more he was putting our leftovers from dinner on this thing he called an altar. He had his grandmother's picture up there. She had died. He would say he is giving her back to his ancestors.

Whatever! All I knew is that he could make good love, cook well, adore me, give me plenty of breathing space, and support when I had to study or work. He would even run baths for me, put rose petals, and different beautiful, rich smelling aromas in the water, and bathe me from head to toe. The rest is left to the imagination. He knew how to tap into my emotions and essences in one sense. However, he abandoned himself in the process. He was so busy trying to put on a facade, because he was fucking a white lady devil. He was actually fucking the pipe. Jesus! When I really knew this man had not grown or could not let go of this addiction no matter how he claimed to love me; the price was too high for both of our souls! He didn't know how to love himself or eradicate the scars of demons hijacking all through him.

That was then. This is now!

I don't know why my mind went back to that time in my life as I hung up on my husband Solomon. He supposedly was a Christian man, "in the name of Jesus" tried to choke the hell out of me, put me in a headlock in front of our son, his oldest sister, her husband, and their teenage son in D.C.

I must be damn delirious. I am standing now in our kitchen, wrapped in

kente cloth almost five months pregnant; wondering when my man, my husband, my friend and lover was coming home to his barefoot, pregnant wife, while holding our son on my hip?
Tears just filled the sink cause I was filled up, tore up….!

I had my husband take Osiris to his grandparents' home. It was time for him to go to my parents house, while I tried to work on our marriage. I am willing. But I damn sure ain't releasing myself to dying. I ain't willing to die to save my marriage! Although I was willing to fight for it, 'cause after all, this was my man, my husband, the father of my children that I consciously consented to in a sound mind.

Little did I know that someone else was creeping in my bed, going through
My clothes, and my family portraits.!
Only if she knew; she had competition.

Looking in the mirror Star began speaking aloud:

"I was too blinded by wanting my family to be glued and silky solid. I did not want to perpetuate the virus of not giving birth to the statistic of the deaths, homicides, and suicides of the black family."

However the season unveils itself at a moment and quick ghost minute in your life that you have to let go, if you do not want to drown. I was drowning for awhile in my own blood; created by a man that I allowed to come into my life. I was the prize who allowed SOLOMON: the privilege, the opportunity to share a vision, dreams, hopes, aspirations, OF MY AffirmationS.

*   *   *   *

Star and her babies had to swim back to land. She now knew what she had to do. She could no longer sigh, and mourn the death of her marriage. She had to dance, choreograph to salsa, merengue, calypso, but most of all she had choreograph to some deep soul, blues, written, sung, and danced by herself.

Mama and daddy was there for her. Star knew in order to survive this mutilation to her spirit, she had to go back down South . She had to go back where it all began. Star had to lock-up in her home in Hampton Virginia and cry and cry and cry. She had to curse, pray, sing, and groan, until it all came out.

Only then, could Mama and Osiris, her first born son came down south to Virginia and help deliver the most beautiful baby girl in the whole wide world;
one who at the time was conceived and pre-planned out of pure soul food, love, Ms. Egypt.

Letter to My Present Seasoned 47-Year-Old Self

The End to Your Beginning. Yes Girl, Black Brown Bronze Girl. You are Jazz Blues that is so right on time to teach lessons learned to encompass and inspire a nation. Perform choreograph your own choreopoem story. Yes Yes Yes Yes Yes snap snap Yes Yes snap!!!

Right on time to see my deep scars on my back where a knife took skin layer with a sharpen one to my abdomen of c section to cut like the night I died on my back with gushing blood of stitches being squeezed from my face and choked from my neck

But This time the knife cut differently so deep in order to save reinvent resurrect anew; How the surgeon's knife took my abdomen to reconstruct my breast from my own skin and tattoo my skin to shape nibbles all from my skin; from me beautiful silky smooth brown skin me; yes in my rear shameless bold bodacious form of stage IV Breast Cancer; Miraculously healed from listening to the ancestral voice of spirit and God hands walking all on top of me inside me with a right on time newly resurrected season. Who would have ever known a little black girl from Harlem With bodacious big dreams and bigger talent and discerned slanted eyes and long natural eyelashes who leaped out from her Queen mother womb to change the world through storytelling her hip hop blues southern news and nakedness bare of modern dance would be challenged with darkness of disease at such an early age encompassing it all at once?

Looking at my younger self I say to my seasoned warrior soldier Goddess Self:
"Let no one stifle you into a molested rape silence by dominating your every essence of sheer black woman in America. The journey cannot be told by others to validate their mishaps or insecure emptiness; so don't you weep baby girl now. You hear child? Cause you are here! You are all woman black bold sacred; no nonsense, fun, elevating, graceful, artistic soul, continue to soar with your wings like an eagle and lioness all wrapped into one! Soar my child. Whoever wants to be a part of the #KMilesJourney
Must do it exclusively on your terms not theirs.

Prof. Keisha R. Miles
#KMilesJOurney
The End to another Amazing Beginning

EPILOGUE

The Unveiling of Skin by first allowing yourself to shed out of layers that stagnate voice but must be told to give voice to silence. There is a season to be still and a time to mourn, love, sigh, reflect, recompress from depression, disease and tell truth to your truth without pushing it further down. Repressing the movements of an experienced revolution, stages of life can no longer become a holiday cancer or untimely death. Time to choreograph the stories into life with poetic lyrical narratives intertwined from the ancestral history past present and future. The collective of poems and narratives of an unveiling the silence that almost went too far and stayed too long. In order to be alive in my authentic DNA as first a Performing Artist of Dance, Acting, Writing, Directing, Choreographing and intertwining it with my gift as an Educational Life Coach could no longer be Silence in the Corner. Time to take Silence Corner to the streets, pulpit, schools and global world. Hopefully inspired readers like yourself will explore layers of issues and self-love as the ultimate audition.

Notes: Silent Corner is the unveiling of mask and shedding of skin.

BIO

Professor Keisha R. Miles is a lifelong educator with a BA in English, a MA in Creative Writing and a MS in Educational Leadership. She is an Educational Life Coach, Professor of English/Drama and a Teacher of the Performing Arts/Humanities for the Department of Education throughout New York. As a performing artist she has produced, written, and choreographed productions for underrepresented children and young adults.

Under Professor Miles' guidance she ensures academic success by getting scholarships for students into top prominent colleges and enrichment programs. She also offers specialized training for teachers and parents to become more effective in providing strategies for their children to achieve higher academic success.

Made in the USA
Middletown, DE
08 December 2020